Richard M. Foxx

DECREASING BEHAVIORS

of Persons With Severe Retardation and Autism

RESEARCH PRESS

2612 North Mattis Avenue
Champaign, Illinois 61821

Decreasing Behaviors of Persons With Severe Retardation and Autism
was originally published under the title *Decreasing Behaviors of Severely Retarded and Autistic Persons.*

To Carrie and Chris for growing up to be such fine individuals with relatively few parental interventions having been required during the process

CONTENTS

PREFACE

This is the second of two volumes for practitioners that cover increasing and decreasing the behaviors of severely and profoundly retarded and autistic individuals. It follows the book on increasing behaviors because of my repeated observation that practitioners often find it more expeditious to decrease rather than increase behavior. Yet the proper approach is first to increase appropriate behavior, so that fewer inappropriate behaviors may remain to be decreased. The text on increasing behavior is intended to provide the reader with a solid behavioral foundation, and is designed to be less complex than this companion volume. This book on decreasing behavior is somewhat more complex since the practitioner must assume greater responsibility when seeking to decrease behavior because of some of the techniques that may be used.

In keeping with the responsibility issue, the material is arranged according to the Least Restrictive Treatment Model so that the techniques described increase in terms of their degree of intrusiveness or restrictiveness. Similarly, the reader begins by learning why accountability is necessary, followed by how to decrease behavior, and then how to evaluate success and maintain it.

This book is intended for teachers, aides, institutional staff, parents, program designers, members of behavior management or restrictive procedures committees, and individuals serving on facility human rights committees. It is not intended for those who have an extensive background in behavioral principles, although they might find it useful for teaching others. It could also be of use in academic settings to supplement a more scholarly text, since it deals with the application of behavioral technology in the "hands-on" world of the overwhelmed practitioner.

In writing a book for such practitioners, I set the following goals. (1) A problem-solving approach would be emphasized that considered the myriad of factors involved in designing effective behavior reduction programs. (2) Only crucial information would be included. (3) The relation between student and practitioner behavior would be stressed. (4) The cookbook approach wherein behavioral recipes are provided would be avoided since such an approach teaches little about understanding behavioral analysis or problem solving. (5) Scientifically based information would be provided that is rarely found in training manuals. For example, in Chapter 4 there is a discussion of extinction-induced aggression and the role it may play in an extinction program. The overall goal, then, was to provide readers with guidelines for analyzing problems and constructing programs to deal effectively with those problems.

Because this book was written to assist readers in either developing effective, humane, and enduring programs or evaluating whether a proposed program meets these criteria, the material is presented whenever possible in nontechnical language in order to maximize its readability. Accordingly, an attempt has been made to strike a fine balance between pragmatic considerations and technical jargon in the text and glossary. I have taken some liberties in defining some of the terms, since I was guided by the observation that highly technical definitions tend to confuse rather than enlighten many practitioners.

Two more explanations are in order. First, the term "student" is used throughout the text even though the various examples reflect residential, home, and classroom situations. This term was chosen because it conveys the spirit of educating and training, whereas words such as "client" and "resident" do not. To me, everyone entrusted with the care of the handicapped is first and foremost a teacher. Thus, the term "teacher" is also frequently used even though the described situation may involve an aide, therapist, psychologist, nurse, or other practitioner. Second, I chose to focus on the severely and profoundly retarded because there are fewer texts available that deal with them. Furthermore, although the focus is on retarded individuals, most of the material is applicable to those autistic individuals who display the same maladaptive behaviors as their retarded counterparts.

I would like to acknowledge the assistance and support of several individuals. My wife, Carolyn, critically read and commented in detail on each chapter. Her contribution was especially appreciated because she took time from her own interests and projects in order to help. Marty McMorrow and Reed Bechtel, two of my colleagues from the Department of Treatment Development at Anna, provided feedback, and Marty deserves special thanks for his help with the glossary and suggested readings. Ellen Morgan did her customary good job of typing my sometimes difficult-to-read handwritten manuscript, and Ron Bittle, the superintendent of the Anna Mental Health and Developmental Center, provided support and encouragement for the project. Finally, I would like to thank the countless practitioners throughout the country who have shared their experiences and insights with me.

Richard M. Foxx
Anna, Illinois

CHAPTER 1

The Least Restrictive Treatment Model

In this book, you'll learn about a number of behaviorally based procedures for decreasing inappropriate behaviors. The procedures are presented according to the Least Restrictive Treatment Model, which was developed to protect developmentally disabled persons' civil liberties. It's very important that this model be understood before the procedures are actually used. We'll explain the purpose and origins of the model in this chapter, and tell you the six guidelines to follow in order to conform to this model. Also, the procedures discussed in this book will be ranked from least to most restrictive.

The Least Restrictive Treatment Model encompasses all aspects of a retarded person's life, including his living environment and the methods used to increase his appropriate behavior and decrease his maladaptive behavior. We'll be concerned here with those techniques that can be used to reduce or eliminate behavior. Within the Least Restrictive Treatment Model, the techniques can be ranked according to their aversiveness, intrusiveness, and severity, beginning with those that are the least aversive and ending with those that are the most aversive. The purpose of the model and this ranking is to ensure that individuals who work with handicapped persons use only those procedures that are necessary and sufficient to eliminate a misbehavior. The model dictates that we can't use a more aversive procedure until we have either demonstrated that a less aversive procedure was ineffective or have conducted a review of the treatment literature that indicates that less aversive procedures have been ineffective in reducing the particular maladaptive behavior in question. Thus, the model guarantees that the least restrictive treatment, that is, the one that is least restrictive of the retarded person's

1

rights, will always be tried first whenever an attempt is made to decrease his misbehavior.

The model was developed just a few years ago as one of the by-products of litigation initiated against institutions for retarded persons. During the course of these lawsuits, it was determined that a number of abuses of retarded persons' civil liberties had occurred. To correct these abuses, some of the following major judicial rulings emerged: (1) retarded persons are entitled, as is everyone, to live in the least restrictive environment, (2) humane and ethically defensible treatment or educational programs must be developed and implemented for retarded persons, and (3) the least restrictive treatment model must be followed when attempts are made to decrease a retarded person's misbehavior. You may recognize that Point 2 was the forerunner of Public Law 94-142 (Education for All Handicapped Children Act) that mandated that all persons of school age were entitled to an education regardless of their handicap. In this book we'll be concerned with the last two points.

STEPS IN FOLLOWING THE MODEL

It's imperative that you understand and follow the Least Restrictive Treatment Model in your facility. By doing so, you'll be providing the best possible educational and treatment opportunities for your students and minimizing the chances that you or your facility will be subject to a lawsuit initiated by a parent or an advocacy group.

To use the model correctly, follow these steps:

1. Take baseline records on the individual's misbehavior (see Chapter 9).
2. Review the treatment literature to determine which procedures have effectively reduced or eliminated the misbehavior.
3. From the successful procedures, choose the least restrictive behavioral treatment procedure and use it for the misbehavior.
4. Collect accurate, reliable records during treatment to determine whether the procedure is effective (see Chapter 10).
5. Only select a more restrictive procedure if your treatment records indicate that the previous procedure was ineffective.
6. When highly aversive procedures are being considered (see Chapters 5-8), always obtain written permission from the stu-

dent's parents, the human rights committee (if your facility has one), and the facility administrator before you implement such procedures.

Now let's look at these steps in detail.

Take baseline records on the individual's misbehavior. Collecting accurate, reliable baseline records of the misbehavior gives you (1) a means of determining the effectiveness of your treatment procedure by comparing the baseline records to the treatment records and (2) a measure of how often the misbehavior occurs prior to treatment. It's important to know the frequency of the misbehavior before treatment in order to design your intervention program. For example, in the next chapter you'll learn about a procedure that involves reinforcing the absence of the misbehavior. In order to know how often to reinforce the absence of the misbehavior, you'll need to know how often it occurs on the average before treatment.

Review the treatment literature to determine which procedures have effectively reduced or eliminated the misbehavior. You can save a great deal of time and trouble by finding out which procedures have already worked with the misbehavior you intend to treat. The treatment literature will tell you, for example, that with rare exceptions all successful treatments of self-abusive behavior included a punishment program (see Chapters 6-8). The treatment literature can be found in the suggested readings at the end of each chapter and in Appendix B which lists journals that publish behavior modification articles.

From the successful procedures, choose the least restrictive behavioral treatment procedure and use it for the misbehavior. Once you know which procedures have been effective in treating the misbehavior, the question then becomes selecting the least restrictive procedure from that group that is most applicable to the student you wish to treat. For instance, given that a punishment procedure will be incorporated into your treatment program for self-abuse, such a procedure will be selected on the basis of (1) its aversiveness and (2) how appropriate it is for the student in question. A child in a preschool program who is occasionally self-abusive will probably require a much less intensive punishment program than an adult living in a state residential facility who is continually restrained and has been exhibiting high rates of self-abuse for years.

Collect accurate, reliable records during treatment to determine whether the procedure is effective. Collecting accurate records during treatment will allow you to determine whether or not the procedure is effective. If the procedure is effective, you'll know that it should be continued. If the procedure is ineffective, you can then either revise it or institute a more restrictive procedure.

Only select a more restrictive procedure if your treatment records indicate that the previous procedure was ineffective. As we just mentioned, you will be justified in implementing a more restrictive procedure if your records show that a less restrictive procedure was ineffective. However, you must allow sufficient time for a procedure to work before it is discarded. In general, the minimum duration for trying a procedure should be between 5 to 10 days or sessions.

When highly aversive procedures are being considered, always obtain written permission from the student's parents, the human rights committee, and the facility administrator before you implement such procedures. The current legal climate dictates that you must obtain permission from all relevant parties to use highly aversive procedures such as physical restraint (Chapter 5) and some of the punishment procedures. An example of how this permission should be sought will be shown next.

EXAMPLE OF A PROGRAM FOLLOWING THE MODEL

The following is an actual program description that was submitted to the student's parents, the institution's human rights committee, and the institution's superintendent. In addition, it was submitted to the state Department of Mental Retardation because an electric shock procedure was proposed as the final treatment procedure. (Permission was granted by everyone to conduct the program. Interestingly, only the first treatment proposed, timeout, was necessary to eliminate the behavior.) The form presented here is modeled after the form used by the Children's Rehabilitation Unit/University Affiliated Facility at the University of Kansas Medical Center for giving informed consent for aversive treatment procedures (Cook, Altman, & Haavik, 1978).

Informed Consent for Aversive Treatment Procedures

Name:_____

Birthdate: _____

Supervisor: _____

Therapists: Richard M. Foxx, Ph.D., _____, _____

I. *Description of Behavior to Be Modified:* The primary behaviors to be modified will be head-banging and nose-banging. Head-banging is defined as occurring whenever any part of either hand (i.e., fist, palm) comes in contact with any part of the head, exclusive of pats or strokes. Nose-banging is defined as occurring whenever the student's hand(s) or knee comes in direct contact with his nose. In the present program, hits to the head and hits to the nose will be counted separately because he has caused the most serious damage to his nose. Also monitored will be thigh-hitting and ankle-kicking. If these latter behaviors appear to be causing harm (tissue damage) they may be targeted for modification at a later date. Thigh-hitting is defined as occurring whenever either hand comes in contact with the thigh, exclusive of pats or strokes. Ankle-kicking is defined as occurring whenever he forcefully brings his two ankles in direct contact.

II. *Description of Treatment Procedures that Have Already Been Implemented:*

1. Ignoring—Tried and found ineffective.
2. Noncontingent restraint (restraint devices)—Reduced severe self-abusive behaviors (head-banging and nose-banging), although the rate of head-banging has recently begun to increase. As soon as the restraints are removed, he begins to self-abuse at a high rate; the results of the blows to his face and nose are readily visible. The use of restraint is primarily for custodial purposes and indefinite periods of restraint are not a desirable treatment alternative. Furthermore, there is sufficient evidence that he finds the restraint devices reinforcing since he asks for them, attempts to restrain himself, and calms down somewhat when they are applied.
3. Timeout—Tried and found ineffective. The student seems to enjoy timeout. He often misbehaves during educational activities he wishes to avoid in order to receive timeout.
4. Modifying his less severe self-abusive behaviors (ankle-kicks, thigh-hits) in a reinforcement room through reinforcement plus tokens, with him wearing his restraints. He participated in reinforcement room activities and did not engage in any mild forms of self-abuse so long as he remained in restraints.

III. *Description of Other Treatment Alternatives:*

1. Heavy sedation—Not desired by parents, institution, or therapists.

2. Overcorrection (Foxx & Azrin, 1972)—His size and strength preclude implementation of this procedure.
3. 24-hour period of social isolation (Foxx, Foxx, Jones, & Kiely, 1980)—He could defeat such a program by becoming extremely combative or self-abusive.

IV. *Justification for Use of Aversive Treatment Procedures:* The student has caused a great deal of physical damage to himself in the past and his self-abusive behavior is a threat to his permanent well-being. His nose is permanently disfigured and actual tissue damage is apparent. Moreover, as a result of his frequent head-banging, he has suffered a number of serious hematomas which are constantly being reinjured. His self-injurious behaviors interfere also with his performance and participation in unit activities. He uses self-abuse to manipulate others. He self-abuses when demands are placed on him, or when he doesn't want to follow instructions or participate. His parents are very concerned and would like the behaviors eliminated. Thus far, none of the procedures described in Section II have been effective in eliminating his self-injurious behaviors. A review of the literature indicates that aversive treatment procedures such as punishment and physical restraint have been most effective in greatly reducing or eliminating self-injurious behavior. The student will continue to receive ongoing reinforcement for appropriate behavior during the treatment sessions.

V. *Description of Aversive Treatment Programs:* The least restrictive treatment model will be followed. Thus, less aversive treatment procedures will be implemented first and more aversive procedures will be added or substituted until a program is found that will eliminate his self-abuse when he is out of restraints. The aversive treatment procedures have been ranked according to the severity of their consequences. They will be combined with reinforcement of alternative appropriate behaviors and the use of his restraints as reinforcers. Since he finds restraint reinforcing, he will be allowed to earn his arm restraints if he does not injure himself for a predetermined period of time. Research has shown that such a method can be successful (Favell, McGimsey, & Jones, 1978).

General Method: The student will be taken to a small session room several times per day for 15 minutes or until his self-abuse becomes so severe that the session must be terminated. His restraints will be removed while he is in the room. The room will have a one-way-vision mirror that will permit the accurate and unobtrusive recording of his behavior. The following conditions will be instituted: *Baseline*—During this condition he will be asked to participate in a variety of educational activities in the room. He will be praised for his efforts at participating. Self-abuse will be recorded and the session terminated as soon as his self-abuse becomes severe. As soon as he calms down, his restraints will be returned and he will be returned to the unit. (We shall require him to become calm before he receives his restraints in order to reduce the possibility that he will associate the return of the restraints with self-injury.) It is anticipated that these self-abusive behaviors will occur more frequently than normal because of the removal of the restraints. *Treatment I* (reinforcement of alternative behaviors, reinforcement of periods of noninjury with restraints, and timeout for self-injury)—In this condition, the same educational demands will be placed on the student as during the baseline, but his efforts to respond and participate will be reinforced with tokens that can later be exchanged for a variety of back-up reinforcers. In addition, he will receive tokens for not self-abusing. He will earn his restraints for a few minutes if he does not injure himself for a specified period. When he does self-abuse he will be removed from the room and required to spend 5 minutes in the unit timeout room. If possible, he will not wear his restraints during the timeout interval. The door will be locked and he will be permitted to leave after 5 minutes, provided that he is calm. If he is agitated, he must remain in the room until he has been calm for at least 1 minute. He will then be returned to the session room. *Treatment II* (reinforcement of appropriate behaviors, reinforcement of periods of noninjury with restraints, and physical restraint for self-injury)—If Treatment I is not effective, then Treatment II will be used. The treatment will consist of the two reinforcement procedures and a physical restraint procedure. Whenever he self-abuses he will be placed on a bed located in the session room and his limbs and torso will be restrained by soft straps. He will be kept in the bed for 15 minutes. *Treatment III*—If Treatment II is ineffective in reducing the self-abuse, then Treatment III will be employed. This treatment will consist of the two reinforcement procedures plus response-contingent electric shock. The response-contingent shock will be delivered by a remote-controlled device. This device has been successfully employed in California by Dr. _____ with more than 20 self-injurious individuals.

VI. *Description of Possible Side Effects:* Possible negative side effects that are associated with any punishment procedure are (1) undesirable emotional reactions, (2) aggression towards the punishing agent, (3) escape and/or avoidance of the punishing situation, and (4) modeled punishment. However, in a review of the literature of the side effects of employing electric shock with autistic children, Lichstein and Schreibman (1976) found that the majority of reported side effects of shock have been of a positive nature. These positive effects included response generalization, increases in social behaviors, and positive emotional behavior (e.g., decreases in whining, crying; increases in smiling, sociability, calmness). The few negative side effects reported included fear of the shock apparatus, negative emotional behavior (e.g., increases in crying, quietness, sullenness), and increases in other maladaptive behavior. (See the attached review of self-injurious behavior and the accompanying scientific publications [not included].)

VII. *Describe Any Special Precautions to Be Used in Implementing the Shock Treatment Procedure:*

1. All safety factors proposed by Butterfield (1975) when using shock will be observed in the present study. (See attached article [not included].)
2. Only staff certified by Dr. Richard Foxx will deliver the shock. No treatment room activities will occur on weekends unless the supervisor is present.

VIII. *Data Recording Procedures:* The frequency of the student's self-abusive behaviors will be recorded during each session. Each minute will be divided into six 10-second intervals and the frequency of his self-abuse will be counted. Reliability of the recording procedures will be assessed intermittently throughout the program by having two observers independently record the frequency of his behavior and by the use of videotape equipment.

IX. *Expected Behavioral Outcome:* It is hoped that self-abuse will be decreased or eliminated at one of the treatment levels. Once his self-abuse is greatly reduced, we will then increase the duration of each treatment session and the length of time he must remain out of restraints in order to earn them. Ultimately we intend to drop the earning of the restraints completely, since wearing them at any time is counter to the spirit of normalization. Finally, in order to demonstrate convincingly that the successful treatment level was responsible for the reduction in self-abuse, it will be necessary to return to an earlier level for just a few sessions. These brief probes will permit us to state unequivocally that the treatment was responsible for the reduction in self-abuse since his self-abuse should be higher during the probes.

Short-Range Goal: The effective treatment should reduce the target behavior within five sessions to less than 10% of the base-line frequency. If not, the next treatment level will be implemented or, in the case of Treatment III, the program will be discontinued.

Long-Range Goal: If an effective treatment is found, the goal will be to reduce self-abusive behavior to zero in both the session room and on the unit. Once self-abuse has been eliminated in the room for several sessions, treatment will begin on the unit using whatever treatment proved to be effective.

Persons Who Will Implement Treatment Procedures:
Richard M. Foxx—Ph.D.

_____—B.A., psychology;
                graduate student in psychology

_____—Program Manager, Building 4

Informed Consent:

1. As legal guardians for _____, we, Mr. and Mrs. _____, hereby consent to the use of the treatment procedures described on the previous pages in the treatment of our son.

2. We acknowledge that no guarantees have been made to us regarding the results of this treatment.

3. We understand that within the scope of this treatment there is no intent to cause detrimental side effects to the patient.

4. We also understand that the treatment procedures described above will be closely monitored and supervised, and in the event of the observation of any side effects which might be in-jurious to the patient, the treatment procedures will be imme-diately terminated. We further understand that the decision to terminate may be made either by ourselves or by the therapist. However, normally the decision will be made jointly.

5. This form has been fully explained to us and we certify that we understand its contents.

   Signature of persons legally authorized to consent for

   _____.

   Address_____
   City & State _____
   Relationship _____
   Date _____

Witness _____

Signature _____

Address _____

City & State _____

References

Butterfield, W. H. Electric shock—safety factors when used for the aversive conditioning of humans. *Behavior Therapy*, 1975, *6*, 98-110.

Cook, J. W., Altman, K., & Haavik, S. Consent for aversive treatment: A model form. *Mental Retardation*, 1978, *16*, 47-51.

Favell, J. E., McGimsey, J. F., & Jones, M. L. The use of physical restraint in the treatment of self-injury and as positive reinforcement. *Journal of Applied Behavior Analysis*, 1978, *11*, 225-241.

Foxx, C. L., Foxx, R. M., Jones, J. R., & Kiely, D. Twenty-four hour social isolation: A program for reducing the aggressive behavior of a psychotic-like retarded adult. *Behavior Modification*, 1980, *4*, 130-144.

Foxx, R. M., & Azrin, N. H. Restitution: A method of eliminating aggressive-disruptive behavior of retarded and brain damaged patients. *Behaviour Research and Therapy*, 1972, *10*, 15-27.

Lichstein, K. L., & Schreibman, L. Employing electric shock with autistic children: A review of the side effects. *Journal of Autism and Childhood Schizophrenia*, 1976, *6*, 163-173.

The message is: document what you intend to do and then document what you are doing. In that way everyone involved clearly knows what is happening, and you avoid legal complications and potential areas of conflict or confusion for parents and staff.

A RANKING OF BEHAVIORAL PROCEDURES ACCORDING TO THE MODEL

As mentioned earlier, the behavioral procedures to decrease behavior can be ranked according to their aversiveness, intrusiveness, and severity. The ranking shown here will be used throughout this book. This ranking is how I would order the procedures and does not necessarily represent how they might be ranked in your state, county, school, or institution. However, based on a number of other rankings, this list seems quite representative.

The procedures are divided into three levels. Level 1 procedures contain no aversive or intrusive properties. As a result, you shouldn't need permission to use them. The sole exception is when satiation is used to treat rumination (see Chapter 3). Level 2 procedures do contain some aversive or intrusive properties or have side effects that dictate caution. Level 2 procedures, therefore, shouldn't be used until parental and administrative permission has been granted. Level 3 procedures can be quite aversive and intrusive, which is why great care must be taken before using them. Permission or consent must be obtained from the student, parents, administrators, and, when appropriate, a human rights and/or restrictive procedures committee.

Level 1	Level 2	Level 3
DRO (Differential Reinforcement of Other Behavior)	Negative practice (when manual guidance is not given)	Negative practice (when manual guidance is given)
DRA (Differential Reinforcement of Appropriate Behavior)	Extinction	Physical restraint
DRI (Differential Reinforcement of Incompatible Behavior)	Nonexclusionary timeout	Exclusionary timeout Overcorrection
Satiation		

The procedures haven't been ranked within the levels because each treatment situation is different. Variables such as the length of the procedure or the baseline frequency of the misbehavior influence whether one procedure within a level would be considered to be more aversive than another. It's suggested that your facility decide how the procedures will be ranked within a level. You don't need to rank the Level 1 procedures, since they are nonaversive.

SUMMARY

The Least Restrictive Treatment Model covers all aspects of a retarded person's life, including the living environment and the techniques used to increase or decrease behaviors. Techniques for decreasing behavior are ranked according to their aversiveness, severity, and intrusiveness to ensure that the least restrictive treatments are always tried first. The model resulted from the major judicial rulings that (1) retarded persons are entitled to live in the least restrictive environment, (2) humane and ethical treatment and educational programs must be created and implemented for the retarded, and (3) the least restrictive treatment must be chosen when trying to decrease a retarded person's inappropriate behavior.

There are six steps in following the Least Restrictive Treatment Model when decreasing misbehaviors. (1) Baseline records of the misbehavior must be taken. (2) The literature must be reviewed to determine which procedures have been used effectively to reduce the misbehavior. (3) The least restrictive procedure must be chosen. (4) Accurate, reliable treatment records must be kept. (5) A more restrictive procedure can be used only if the first treatment fails. (6) Written consent or permission for the use of highly aversive procedures must be obtained from the student (when appropriate), parents, the facility administrator, and the human rights committee, if there is one.

The procedures described in this book are ranked from least to most restrictive by three levels. Level 1 procedures have no aversive or intrusive properties; Level 2 procedures have some; Level 3 procedures are quite aversive and intrusive, and require written permission before use. Each institution should decide how to rank the procedures within Levels 2 and 3.

SUGGESTED READINGS

Birnbrauer, J. S. Some guides to designing behavioral programs. In D. Marholin II (Ed.), *Child behavior therapy*. New York: Gardner Press, 1978.

Heads, T. B. Ethical and legal considerations in behavior therapy. In D. Marholin II (Ed.), *Child behavior therapy*. New York: Gardner Press, 1978.

May, J. G., Risley, T. R., Twardosz, S., Friedman, P., Bijou, S., & Wexler, D. *Guidelines for the use of behavioral procedures in state programs for retarded persons*. Arlington, Tex.: National Association for Retarded Citizens, 1976.

Review Set 1

1. One of the features of the L_____ R_____ T_____ M_____ is that procedures to reduce behaviors are ranked according to their aversiveness, severity, and intrusiveness.

2. The development of the Least Restrictive Treatment Model was a by-product of l_____ against institutions for retarded persons.

3. There are six steps to follow in using the Least Restrictive Treatment Model: (a) take a b_____ of the student's misbehavior, (b) review the treatment l_____ to determine which procedures have been effective, (c) choose the l_____ restrictive behavioral intervention that the literature indicates has been successful, (d) collect a_____, reliable treatment records, (e) only select a more/less restrictive procedure if the treatment data indicate that the more/less restrictive procedure was ineffective (Circle the correct answers), (f) when considering the use of a highly aversive procedure, always obtain written permission from the individual's p_____, the h_____ r_____ committee, the individual when appropriate, and the facility's a_____ before implementing the procedure.

4. The procedures discussed in this book are ranked into t_____ levels from least to most restrictive.

Answers are found on page 163.

CHAPTER 2

Reinforcement Procedures

The least restrictive procedures for decreasing behavior involve the use of reinforcement procedures. It's highly unlikely that you would ever encounter any legal problems as a result of using reinforcement procedures to decrease misbehaviors. (In fact, I know of no institution or school district that requires approval to use a reinforcement procedure to decrease a misbehavior.) There are three reinforcement procedures that will be discussed: DRO (Differential Reinforcement of Other Behavior); DRA (Differential Reinforcement of Appropriate Behavior) or RAB (Reinforcement of Appropriate Behavior); and DRI (Differential Reinforcement of Incompatible Behavior) or RIB (Reinforcement of Incompatible Behavior). You'll learn the advantages and disadvantages of each and the rules to follow in administering them, including the three rules for designing a reduction program and the cardinal rule for using reinforcement to decrease behavior.

Before we begin discussing the various procedures, let's briefly review reinforcers and reinforcement. A *reinforcer* is any event that maintains or increases the future occurrence of the behavior it follows. If an event is to be a reinforcer, it must be something the student likes and for which she will respond. When a reinforcer is delivered following the student's behavior, it is called a *reinforcing consequence*, since it will increase the likelihood that the behavior will increase in frequency, that is, occur more often in the future. Simply put, *reinforcement* is the procedure by which a reinforcer is delivered following a behavior, thus strengthening that behavior. The teacher's action of providing a reinforcer or using reinforcement is called *reinforcing* the behavior. The term reinforcing can also describe an event that has proven to be a reinforcer, as in the statement "Dick finds praise reinforcing." A listing of potential reinforcers can be found in Appendix A. In this chapter you will learn how reinforcement can be used to decrease maladaptive behaviors by strengthening other behaviors.

DRO (DIFFERENTIAL REINFORCEMENT
OF OTHER BEHAVIOR)

> DRO (Differential Reinforcement of Other Behavior) is a procedure in which a reinforcer is given at the end of a specified interval provided that a prespecified misbehavior has not occurred during the interval.

DRO is perhaps the simplest of all reductive procedures. In a DRO procedure you're *reinforcing the absence of the misbehavior.* All you have to determine is whether or not the misbehavior occurred. The following example illustrates the correct use of a DRO procedure.

Robby is a 10-year-old severely retarded boy who engages in self-abusive behavior. He self-abuses by repeatedly striking the sides of his head with his fists throughout the school day. His teacher, Ms. Hodos, decides to use a DRO procedure to reduce Robby's self-abuse. Ms. Hodos' first task is to determine how often Robby hits himself. She does so by continuously observing Robby for 5 minutes each half hour and recording each blow to the head. After conducting a brief, 3-day baseline, Ms. Hodos finds that Robby hits himself on the average of about once every 30 seconds. Based on this information, Ms. Hodos makes five important decisions: (1) she'll set the DRO interval at 15 seconds, (2) she'll only use the DRO procedure with Robby during a half-hour period each day, (3) she'll conduct the session on a one-to-one basis behind a partition in the classroom, (4) she'll entertain Robby with a variety of toys and play objects during the session, and (5) she'll select Robby's most preferred reinforcer, potato sticks, as the reinforcer for not hitting.

During the sessions, Ms. Hodos is seated at a table across from Robby. Every time 15 seconds elapses without Robby having hit himself, Ms. Hodos says, "Good, Robby, you didn't hit yourself" and places a potato stick in his mouth. Once Robby hasn't hit himself for a few days (two or three) during the 15-second DRO procedure, Ms. Hodos increases the DRO interval to 30 seconds. When a few days have passed without any hits, Ms.

Hodos increases the DRO interval to 1 minute. She continues to increase the DRO interval until Robby can go 15 minutes without hitting himself. At that point she begins using the 15-minute DRO procedure throughout the 6-hour school day.

Ms. Hodos' use of the DRO procedure was perfect because she carefully planned how she would use the procedure. The five decisions she made were extremely important in making the program a success. Let's examine why.

Ms. Hodos' first decision followed the cardinal rule in using a DRO procedure: *always select an initial DRO interval that is at least half as short as the average interval of the inappropriate behavior.* Ms. Hodos selected 15 seconds as the initial DRO interval because Robby normally hit himself every 30 seconds. She thus ensured that the initial DRO interval was half as long as the average interval between hits.

Her next three decisions followed the general rules necessary to keep the program consistent. These general rules for designing any program to decrease behavior are:

1. *Select a time period each day that can be devoted completely to the student's program.* Ms. Hodos limited the DRO program to one half hour per day, which ensured that the program would be consistent since she could afford to devote that much time to Robby's program.

2. *Have one person take responsibility for the program.* Ms. Hodos used a one-to-one approach with herself as the only change or treatment agent. By doing this, she eliminated the possibility that there would be any inconsistencies across change agents.

3. *Create activities that are as incompatible as possible with the inappropriate behavior.* Robby was provided with a variety of toys and objects during the session. The distraction function of these objects increased the likelihood that Robby would be able to go for 15 seconds without hitting himself.

Ms. Hodos' fifth and final decision followed one of the cardinal rules in using any reinforcement procedure: *always select the most preferred (powerful) reinforcer available.* She selected potato sticks as the reinforcer because they are Robby's favorite food and would therefore ensure that Robby's motivation to not hit himself would be as high as possible. You'll see the application of this reinforcement rule and the rules for programmatic consistency throughout this book.

Two advantages of using a DRO procedure are:

1. It's an easy procedure to use. All you have to do is determine whether or not the misbehavior occurred.
2. You're working directly on the misbehavior by reinforcing its absence.

However, there are two disadvantages associated with using a DRO procedure:

1. The procedure isn't designed to teach or increase any appropriate behaviors.
2. You're committed to reinforcing the student at the end of the DRO interval, provided that the misbehavior has not occurred. And in doing so, you run the risk of reinforcing other types of inappropriate behavior. For example, consider the following situation. Robby has gone 15 seconds without hitting himself. Just as Ms. Hodos places the potato stick in his mouth, Robby throws a toy. What has Ms. Hodos reinforced? She may have just reinforced object throwing, which is clearly an inappropriate behavior. Regardless of whether or not object throwing is less appropriate than self-abuse, it's undesirable. Thus, we see one of the inherent limitations of the DRO procedure. To overcome this limitation, it's best to *specify any other behaviors that will not be followed by the reinforcer.* It's better to let a DRO interval pass without delivering a reinforcer than to reinforce an inappropriate behavior.

Practice Set 2A

Answer the following questions.

1. After taking a baseline, Ms. Arthur found that Shari bites her hand every 20 seconds. Ms. Arthur should set the DRO interval at _____.
2. Mr. Ryan is using a DRO procedure of 15 minutes to treat Karen's screaming. At the end of the 15-minute interval, Karen rips her blouse just as Mr. Ryan is about to give her an edible reinforcer and praise for not screaming during the interval. Should Mr. Ryan reinforce Karen? Why?
3. Ms. Warren, the mother of one of your students, asks you to help design a home program for her daughter. What three general rules would you tell her to follow to ensure consistency in the program?

4. You'd like Ms. Walters to try a DRO procedure in her class-room. Accordingly, you'll tell her about the advantages and disadvantages of the procedure. What two advantages will you discuss? What two disadvantages will you caution her about?

5. Dante, a saliva smearer, likes physical contact with an aide more than edible reinforcers or praise. If you decided to use a DRO procedure to reduce Dante's smearing, what would you use as a reinforcer? Why?

The answers are on pages 163 and 164.

DRA (DIFFERENTIAL REINFORCEMENT OF APPROPRIATE BEHAVIOR)

> DRA (Differential Reinforcement of Appropriate Behavior) is a procedure in which a reinforcer is given following the performance of a prespecified appropriate behavior.

The DRA (Differential Reinforcement of Appropriate Behavior) or RAB (Reinforcement of Appropriate Behavior) procedure specifies an appropriate behavior to be increased by reinforcement. As a result, the first disadvantage of DRO—that appropriate behaviors are not being increased—is eliminated. Furthermore, DRA minimizes the second disadvantage of DRO, since there is little chance that an inappropriate behavior will be increased.

The rationale for using a DRA procedure to decrease behavior is that increasing an appropriate behavior may produce a simultaneous decrease in the targeted inappropriate behavior. In essence, you're hoping to increase the student's performance of the appropriate behavior to a point where he has little, if any, time or inclination to perform the inappropriate behavior. The following example illustrates the correct use of a DRA procedure.

Ms. Hodos has decided to use a DRA procedure to reduce Robby's self-abuse. After taking a baseline of Robby's hitting, she decides that a good behavior to increase would be Robby's eye contact. She decided to use eye contact because Robby would occasionally look at someone when instructed to do so. Ms. Hodos arranges to give Robby two 15-minute eye contact training sessions per day. The training will be one-to-one and will be conducted at a table behind a partition. Ms. Hodos will use bite-sized bits of potato sticks to reinforce eye contact. She will not bring any objects into the training area because they might distract Robby during the training sessions.

During the sessions Ms. Hodos sits directly across the table from Robby. She takes a piece of potato stick out of a bowl located to her right (and out of Robby's reach) and moves the potato stick toward her eye. As Robby begins tracking the potato stick with his eyes, Ms. Hodos says, just as the potato stick reaches her eye, "Robby, look at me." When Robby's eyes make brief contact with her eyes, Ms. Hodos says, "Good, Robby, you looked at me" and places the potato stick in his mouth. Ms. Hodos then lightly strokes the side of his face and says once again, "Good, Robby, you looked at me." She then records Robby's correct response, after which she begins another trial. Over time she finds that Robby's rate of looking at her has increased and that his frequency of hitting his head has decreased. Eventually Ms. Hodos plans to require Robby to look at her for a full 2 seconds when instructed to do so and to gradually reduce and eliminate the use of the potato stick near her eyes. Later she'll add other educational activities to the sessions as well as using these activities during the entire school day.

Ms. Hodos used the DRA procedure quite effectively and it accomplished its intended purpose: Robby's eye contact increased and his self-abuse decreased. Ms. Hodos followed the rules necessary to ensure the consistency and success of any program designed to decrease an inappropriate behavior (see page 17), the cardinal rule for using a reinforcement procedure, that is, select a powerful reinforcer, and finally the cardinal rule when using a DRA procedure: *always select a behavior to increase that the student already performs*. This, of course, is why Ms. Hodos chose eye contact as the behavior to increase.

DRA is the procedure to use whenever you want to increase a behavior regardless of whether or not any misbehaviors are occurring. During its use most other behaviors, either appropriate or inappropriate, will often decrease in frequency because of the increase in frequency of the reinforced behavior.

The advantage of using a DRA procedure to decrease a misbehavior is that an appropriate behavior is increased. Thus, it allows you to incorporate a part of the student's educational program into a program to decrease a misbehavior. However, there are two disadvantages associated with the DRA procedure:

1. DRA doesn't directly affect the misbehavior.
2. The misbehavior can still occur. For example, Robby could still hit himself during the eye contact training sessions. In

fact, he could hit himself and look at Ms. Hodos simultaneously. (If this happened, Ms. Hodos should not reinforce the eye contact, but rather should ignore the hit, wait for hitting to stop, and then resume the eye contact training. Otherwise, she would run the risk of reinforcing hitting.)

What can you do to remedy these inherent disadvantages of DRA? The answer can be found in the discussion of DRI, the third reinforcement procedure for reducing a misbehavior.

Practice Set 2B

Answer the following questions.

1. Ms. Goldman would like to use a DRA procedure with Teddy, who rocks a good deal of the time. Teddy does respond to simple commands such as "Look at me" and "Give me the (object)." Ms. Goldman also has been considering teaching Teddy to point to objects. She is undecided as to which appropriate behavior she should choose to reinforce. Which behavior(s) should she pick?

2. You would like Mr. Battle to try a DRA procedure at home with his daughter. What will you tell him is the advantage of the procedure? What two disadvantages will you describe?

3. Mr. Henson has been reinforcing Jerry every 10 minutes for not belching. Although this program has been successful, Mr. Henson is concerned that Jerry is not displaying enough appropriate behaviors. What could Mr. Henson do to answer this concern? What type of procedure was he using initially?

Answers are found on page 164.

DRI (DIFFERENTIAL REINFORCEMENT OF INCOMPATIBLE BEHAVIOR)

DRI (Differential Reinforcement of Incompatible Behavior) is a procedure in which a reinforcer is given following the performance of a prespecified appropriate behavior that is physically and functionally incompatible with the targeted inappropriate behavior.

The DRI procedure (Differential Reinforcement of Incompatible Behavior) or RIB (Reinforcement of Incompatible Behavior) offers you the greatest reinforcement control over the inappropriate behavior. This control comes because the appropriate and inappropriate behaviors cannot occur simultaneously since they are physically and functionally incompatible. In effect, DRI is a combination of DRO and DRA.

The rationale for using a DRI procedure is that increasing the targeted incompatible appropriate behavior guarantees that the inappropriate behavior will decrease in frequency. Under ideal conditions there should be no opportunity for the student to perform the inappropriate behavior if the appropriate behavior occurs often enough. The following example illustrates the correct use of a DRI procedure.

Ms. Hodos has decided to use a DRI procedure to reduce Robby's hitting his head with his fists. She decides that the best incompatible behavior to reinforce would be one that kept Robby's hands on the table and away from his head. The behavior she selects is having Robby scribble on a piece of paper because he has performed this behavior in the past. Ms. Hodos plans to have Robby hold the paper on the table with the flat of his left hand and scribble with a crayon held in his right hand. Robby can only obtain a reinforcer if both of his hands are in contact with the paper. Ms. Hodos arranges to give Robby four 15-minute "coloring" sessions behind a partition. No other materials or persons will be present in the session area. Bits of potato sticks will be used to reinforce the scribbling.

During the sessions Ms. Hodos sits beside Robby. She begins by guiding his left hand to the paper and his right hand in a scribbling or coloring motion. Within a second or two, Ms. Hodos pops a bit of potato stick into Robby's mouth, simultaneously says, "Good coloring, Robby," and then caresses Robby's cheek as she repeats the phrase. Over time Ms. Hodos increases the duration between reinforcers from 3 seconds to 5 seconds to 10 seconds, and so forth, until Robby will color for 3 minutes between reinforcers. Since Ms. Hodos paced Robby very carefully, only a few blows to the head occurred.

When Robby is coloring for 3 minutes in order to receive praise and a bit of a potato stick, Ms. Hodos begins introducing new activities into the session that require Robby to use both his hands. She begins reinforcing Robby every few seconds for performing these activities and then gradually increases the interval between reinforcers as she had done for the scribbling. After Robby performs a variety of incompatible activities for the reinforcer every 3 minutes, Ms. Hodos returns Robby to the classroom, where the activities will be scheduled to occur during the day. After a few days in which no hitting occurs in the classroom, Ms. Hodos plans to schedule some activities for Robby that do not have to be incompatible with his hitting.

Ms. Hodos did an excellent job of conducting the DRI procedure. Robby's hitting was reduced quickly because he had learned that when he did hit, he forfeited the opportunity to be reinforced because his hands had left the table. Ms. Hodos followed all the rules previously mentioned for using a reinforcement procedure to decrease a misbehavior. And she followed the cardinal rule in using the DRI procedure: *always select a behavior to increase (reinforce) that is physically and functionally incompatible with the misbehavior and one that the student already performs.*

The major advantage of the DRI procedure is that the inappropriate behavior can't happen when the incompatible behavior is occurring. This aspect of DRI provides you with the greatest possible reinforcement control over the misbehavior since, if the reinforcer is powerful enough and the response requirement for achieving it is reasonable, the student has little motivation to perform the misbehavior.

The major disadvantage of the DRI procedure is that it's sometimes difficult to find an appropriate, incompatible behavior. Finding an incompatible behavior is difficult enough, but finding one that is also appropriate can require a good deal of thought and creativity. For instance, consider the kinds of incompatible behaviors that could have been selected for Robby. Several possibilities include having Robby sit on his hands, keep his hands in his pockets, keep his hands flat on the table, keep his hands in his lap, interlock his fingers and keep his hands on the table, or hold onto an object with both hands. All of these behaviors are incompatible with hitting his head with his hands, yet none would be appropriate for Robby to perform for very long. If he performed them for long periods, he would not be performing or learning anything that would raise his level of functioning. However, the incompatible behavior that was selected, scribbling, offered the advantages of increasing Robby's motor coordination while also being developmentally appropriate. *Remember, when using DRI, it is important to select a behavior not only for its incompatibility with the misbehavior, but also for its social and educational appropriateness.* Sometimes this is difficult to do, but it's a goal worth attempting.

Practice Set 2C

Answer the following questions.

1. Here is a list of incompatible behaviors that could be rein-

forced with a DRI procedure. Match the incompatible behaviors on the right to the inappropriate behaviors on the left.

1____putting hand in mouth   a. placing pegs in pegboard
2____shouting   b. urinating in the toilet
3____running around the room   c. putting hand on table
4____urinating on the floor   d. keeping clothing on
5____removing clothing   e. remaining quiet
6____throwing pegs   f. sitting in a chair

2. You're giving an in-service workshop to institutional staff. What will you tell them is the advantage of a DRI procedure? What disadvantage will you describe?

3. Which of the three reinforcement procedures would be most appropriate to use in treating self-abusive behavior?

4. Here are some examples of the use of reinforcement procedures to decrease a misbehavior. Identify which reinforcement procedure is being used.

   a. A child is allowed to watch TV as long as her thumb remains out of her mouth. _____

   b. Jock is frequently out of his chair. His teacher begins a program in which she reinforces Jock for remaining in his seat. _____

   c. Peter picks at his face with his fingers. The occupational therapist begins reinforcing Peter's correct identification of pictures of common objects. _____

   d. Jose, a screamer, receives a reinforcer every 20 seconds for being quiet. _____

   e. Dorothy receives a sip of cola every 2 minutes if she has not removed her clothes. _____

   f. Arnie, a drooler, receives a reinforcer every 15 seconds for working on a puzzle. _____

The answers are on pages 164 and 165.

RELATIVE EFFECTIVENESS OF THE PROCEDURES

Of the three reinforcement procedures, DRI will usually produce the greatest reductions in the misbehavior. This, of course, is because if the DRI program is successful, the misbehavior must decrease because it's incompatible with the appropriate behavior that has been increased. Under ideal conditions, DRI can reduce the misbehavior to zero. As a rule, you can expect DRO and DRA procedures to produce about a 50% decrease in a misbehavior relative to its baseline level. Greater reductions are possible when DRO and DRA are combined with some of the more intrusive reductive procedures that will be described in later chapters.

SUMMARY

There are three reinforcement procedures that can be used for decreasing inappropriate behaviors: DRO (Differential Reinforcement of Other Behavior), DRA (Differential Reinforcement of Appropriate Behavior), and DRI (Differential Reinforcement of Incompatible Behavior). When conducted properly, none of the three restrict the retarded person's rights.

DRO is a procedure in which the absence of misbehavior is reinforced following a specified interval of time. The initial DRO interval must always be at least half as short as the average interval of the misbehavior. DRO is the simplest reinforcement procedure, and it works directly on the misbehavior; however, it doesn't increase an appropriate behavior, and care must be taken not to inadvertently reinforce some other inappropriate behavior.

DRA is a procedure in which a specific appropriate behavior is reinforced. It must be a behavior that the student already performs. Although DRA increases an appropriate behavior, it doesn't work directly on the misbehavior being treated and doesn't prevent the misbehavior from occurring.

DRI is a procedure in which a behavior is reinforced that is physically and functionally incompatible with the inappropriate behavior. When using DRI, it's very important to select an incompatible behavior that is socially and educationally relevant and that the student already performs. DRI offers the greatest reinforcement control of the three reinforcement procedures because the misbehavior and incompatible behavior can't occur simultaneously.

The three general rules to follow in designing any program to decrease behavior are to (1) select a time period that can be devoted exclusively to the program, (2) have one person take responsibility for the program, and, (3) in general, create activities that are incompatible with the inappropriate behavior. A cardinal rule for all reinforcement programs is to always use the most preferred reinforcer available.

Of the three reinforcement procedures, DRI usually reduces misbehavior most effectively. DRO and DRA procedures can produce about a 50% decrease in a misbehavior, but this percentage can be raised by combining them with more intrusive reductive procedures.

SUGGESTED READINGS

Bostow, D. E., & Bailey, J. B. Modification of severe disruptive and aggressive behavior using brief timeout and reinforcement procedures. *Journal of Applied Behavior Analysis*, 1969, *2*, 31-38.

Corte, H. E., Wolf, M. M., & Locke, B. J. A comparison of procedures for eliminating self-injurious behavior of retarded adolescents. *Journal of Applied Behavior Analysis*, 1971, *4*, 201-214.

Foxx, R. M. Weight reduction in an obese retarded adolescent through social reinforcement. *Mental Retardation*, 1972, *10*, 21-23.

Foxx, R. M., & Azrin, N. H. The elimination of autistic self-stimulatory behavior by overcorrection. *Journal of Applied Behavior Analysis*, 1973, *6*, 1-14.

Myers, D. V. Extinction, DRO, and response-cost procedures for eliminating self-injurious behavior: A case study. *Behaviour Research and Therapy*, 1975, *13*, 189-192.

Repp, A. C., & Dietz, S. M. Reducing aggressive and self-injurious behavior of institutionalized retarded children through reinforcement of other behavior. *Journal of Applied Behavior Analysis*, 1974, *7*, 313-325.

Review Set 2

1. A D_____ procedure is used when you reinforce the absence of the misbehavior following a specified interval of time.

2. The cardinal rule in using DRO is that the DRO interval must always be at least h_____ as s_____ as the average interval between occurrences of the inappropriate behavior.

3. One advantage of a DRO procedure is that it is so s_____.

4. Another advantage of DRO is that it works d_____ on the misbehavior.

5. The two disadvantages of a DRO procedure are that (a) no a_____ behaviors are taught, and (b) there is a

possibility that an i_____ behavior may be reinforced at the end of the DRO interval.

6. To overcome the second disadvantage of DRO, it's best to specify any b_____ that will not be followed by a reinforcer.

7. A D_____ procedure is used when a reinforcer is given following the performance of a prespecified appropriate behavior.

8. DRA is also known as R_____.

9. By increasing an appropriate behavior with a DRA procedure, you hope that the student will have less time to perform the i_____ behavior.

10. The advantage of a DRA procedure is that a specific a_____ behavior is increased. This allows you to incorporate a part of the individual's educational program into a program to decrease inappropriate behavior.

11. One disadvantage of DRA is that the i_____ behavior can still occur. A second disadvantage is that the procedure doesn't work d_____ on the misbehavior.

12. A D_____ procedure is when a reinforcer is given following the performance of a prespecified appropriate behavior that's physically and functionally i_____ with the inappropriate behavior.

13. Another name for DRI is R_____.

14. The advantage of a DRI procedure is that the i_____ behavior can't occur when the incompatible appropriate behavior is occurring.

15. The disadvantage of DRI is that it is often difficult to find an i_____ behavior that is socially and educationally relevant.

16. The three general rules to follow in designing a program to reduce behavior are to (a) select a t_____ period that can be devoted exclusively to the program, (b) have one p_____ take responsibility for the program, and, (c) in general, create activities that are i_____ with the inappropriate behavior.

17. The cardinal rule for using any reinforcement procedure to decrease behavior is to always select the most powerful r_____ possible.

18. The cardinal rule in using a DRA or DRI procedure is to always select a behavior to increase that the student already p_____.

19. Of the three reinforcement procedures, D_____ produces the greatest reductions in the misbehavior.

Answers are found on page 165.

CHAPTER 3

Satiation and Negative Practice

In the preceding chapter you learned about reinforcement procedures as one way to decrease inappropriate behaviors. In this chapter you'll be introduced to two more reductive procedures: satiation and negative practice. We'll tell you how to do each procedure and point out the advantages and disadvantages of each. Since the procedures are similar, they are sometimes confused, so we'll also show you the specific ways in which they differ from one another. At the end, the procedures given so far in this book will be ranked according to the Least Restrictive Treatment Model.

SATIATION

> Satiation is a procedure in which a reinforcer that has been maintaining a misbehavior is presented noncontingently in unlimited amounts in order to reduce that behavior.

The satiation procedure is appropriate for only a few types of misbehavior. To understand how and why a satiation procedure works, recall that satiation occurs when a reinforcer has been presented to the point where it's no longer effective in increasing or maintaining a behavior. Since a misbehavior occurs because some type of reinforcer follows it, you can use satiation to reduce a misbehavior by simply determining what reinforcer maintains the misbehavior and then providing unlimited access to that reinforcer before the misbehavior occurs. In effect, the student doesn't have to misbehave in order to obtain the reinforcer because he either has received large amounts of it or prolonged exposure to it. The misbehavior is reduced because the student isn't motivated (there's no deprivation from the reinforcer) to perform it. The following example illustrates how satiation works.

Fred steals food from the other students. He waits until someone isn't looking, and then grabs that person's food. Fred's misbehavior is stealing food and the reinforcer for this behavior is probably the food (the reinforcer also could be attention from the staff or other students). What would happen if Fred were given as much food to eat at each meal as he desired? Would Fred still steal food? The answer depends on what reinforcer is maintaining his food stealing. If food were the reinforcer, the stealing would stop, because Fred would be full (satiated on food) and therefore would have no motivation to steal. Of course, if he continued to steal food but didn't eat it, we could state with confidence that attention was probably the reinforcer maintaining food stealing. In that case we'd probably want to use a reductive technique other than satiation to decrease food stealing. Regardless of which reductive technique we chose, however, we would have identified the reinforcer for food stealing.

The most important points to remember in using a satiation procedure to reduce a misbehavior are:

1. Always provide large quantities of the reinforcer or lengthy exposure to it *before* the student has had a chance to misbehave. Otherwise you run the risk of reinforcing the misbehavior if you follow it with the reinforcer. *Remember, in a satiation procedure, the reinforcer is always presented independent of and prior to the misbehavior or noncontingently.*

2. Always make sure that you've identified the specific reinforcer that's maintaining the misbehavior.

As mentioned earlier, there are very few misbehaviors for which a satiation procedure is appropriate. Most people are understandably hesitant to use a procedure that involves providing the reinforcer that has been maintaining the misbehavior. As a result, satiation has been used mostly for misbehaviors related to food or those that are annoying but not a serious threat to the person or others. For instance, satiation has been used to treat food stealing (as in the previous example), rumination, clothes tearing or ripping, and hoarding.

An especially interesting use of satiation is in the treatment of rumination. Rumination is a maladaptive behavior in which the person regurgitates (vomits) and then either chews and reswallows the vomitus or expels it from his mouth. In either case, the individual usually ruminates repeatedly for up to 45 minutes or so after each meal. If the person expels the vomitus, a serious health hazard may arise because vital nutrients are being lost. In fact, the situation can become life threatening since the person is retaining little, if any, food in his stomach. Such individuals often look emaciated and are almost always hospitalized. Fortunately life-threatening rumination is somewhat rare and there's only a remote chance that you'll encounter it in your classroom or living unit. Nonlife-threatening rumination, when the vomitus is reswallowed, is, unfortunately, not uncommon in classrooms and residential facilities for severely and profoundly retarded persons. Although this rumination doesn't present a major health hazard, there are problems associated with the behavior. The ruminator is unsightly; he usually has some vomitus on his clothing and around his mouth, smells bad, and may have irritated skin around his lips and face due to the moist and acidic vomitus. Furthermore, rumination is a form of self-stimulation since it is repetitive, nonfunctional, and interferes with learning. This is the major reason rumination cannot be tolerated in the classroom or during behavioral programming.

Treating nonlife-threatening rumination with a satiation procedure is simply a matter of providing the ruminator with double or triple portions of his meal; in other words, allowing the ruminator to eat until he is full (satiated). If this is done, the person's rumination following the meal generally decreases by anywhere from 50 to 90%. The rumination is decreased because the reinforcer for rumination is the sensation produced by food in the stomach. In essence, the ruminator is still hungry following the meal and engages in behaviors such as chewing and swallowing vomitus because they lead to the sensations of food in the stomach. However, the person is not motivated to ruminate (misbehave) when large amounts of the reinforcer (food) are delivered noncontingently (independent of and prior to the misbehavior) because of the increased number of stomach sensations that are produced. You've probably guessed the major concerns associated with using satiation to treat rumination: the possibility that the student will gain weight, and the amount of food required. Therefore, accurate records of the student's weight and food consumed at each meal must be kept.

The major advantage of satiation is that it is a nonaversive and nonintrusive procedure. As such it permits the instructor or therapist to decrease the student's misbehavior without resorting to a more intrusive procedure. Thus, satiation is considered to be a Level 1 procedure in the Least Restrictive Model of Treatment.

However, research has shown that, in general, misbehaviors treated by satiation are not eliminated until a more aversive procedure such as punishment is coupled with the satiation procedure.

There are several disadvantages associated with the use of satiation:

1. The procedure is rarely, if ever, completely effective in eliminating the undesirable behavior.

2. It's only temporarily effective because the effects of satiation will wane and deprivation will begin to occur.

3. There's always the danger that the reinforcer will be delivered following the misbehavior, rather than independent of or prior to the misbehavior, thereby reinforcing and strengthening it.

4. There are many undesirable behaviors for which a satiation procedure is not appropriate because of the potential dangers associated with delivering the reinforcers that have been maintaining the misbehavior. For example, you would hardly consider using satiation to treat self-abuse, aggressive behavior towards others, or many other forms of highly disruptive behavior.

In summary, great care should be exercised when you consider the use of satiation. To prevent any problems, always make sure that (1) you have determined the reinforcer that's maintaining the undesirable behavior and (2) you deliver the reinforcers independent of (prior to) the misbehavior.

Practice Set 3A

Answer the following questions.

1. For which of the following misbehaviors would it be reasonable to try a satiation procedure?

Climbing on chairs   Self-stimulatory rocking
Masturbating in public   Hoarding toys
Stealing toys   Screaming in the classroom
Air swallowing   Banging tables with a toy

2. Ms. Harris would like to try satiation to treat her student's hoarding of his dirty clothes in his closet on the living unit. What would you suggest that she do in order to use satiation correctly?

3. Travis engages in nonlife-threatening rumination in the classroom following lunch. If you choose to treat his rumination with a food satiation procedure, what will you do? What

two safeguards will you follow? What is your rationale for choosing to treat Travis' rumination by satiation?

The answers are on pages 165 and 166.

NEGATIVE PRACTICE

> Negative practice is a procedure in which the misbehaving person is required to repeatedly practice her inappropriate behavior.

Negative practice has been used most often in treating normal individuals who wish to reduce annoying habits such as nail biting, facial and body tics (such as eye blinking, facial grimacing, and body jerking), and stuttering. The procedure basically consists of simply instructing the person to practice the habit repeatedly during a specified period of time. If these instructions are followed religiously, there is sometimes a subsequent decrease in the frequency of the habit.

Negative practice has been used by therapists to decrease the misbehaviors of retarded persons, but only in a few instances. There are several reasons why.

Retarded persons typically will not practice their misbehaviors when instructed to do so because they are not as motivated as normal persons to eliminate inappropriate behaviors from their behavioral repertoires. This lack of motivation results, in large part, from their behavioral and intellectual deficits. With so few appropriate behaviors that can receive reinforcement, their inappropriate behaviors often become their main source of obtaining reinforcement in the form of some powerful reinforcer such as attention. Normal individuals, of course, usually don't have this problem since they have an elaborate behavioral repertoire that leads to many varied sources of attention. Because the retarded individual is usually unwilling to engage in negative practice, she must be physically guided so that she'll perform the misbehavior. As you can guess, such a physical encounter between the student and a staff member can lead to some serious problems that will be discussed shortly.

Staff members often feel uncomfortable, and rightly so, with the idea of requiring the student to perform the inappropriate behavior. The general feeling is that it's difficult enough to reduce or eliminate an inappropriate behavior without attempting to do so by giving the student opportunities to practice and possibly refine her inappropriate behavior.

There are only a few misbehaviors to which negative practice is applicable. For example, you certainly wouldn't use negative practice to treat aggressive behaviors, self-abuse, or disruptive behaviors, and the potentially hazardous consequences of doing so can be easily imagined.

Although there are disadvantages associated with the use of negative practice, there are a few situations when negative practice could be an effective treatment procedure. The rationale for using negative practice is that the physical effort involved in repeatedly performing the misbehavior will become so aversive that the student will stop misbehaving in order to avoid the negative practice consequence. The following example illustrates the correct use of a negative practice procedure.

Brenda is a 16-year-old severely retarded student who frequently rips her clothing at both school and home. Her instructors are greatly concerned about Brenda's ripping because it's costly, interferes with their educational efforts, and makes it chancy, at best, to take her on field trips. They feel that Brenda's ripping is maintained by the attention she receives following a ripping episode. In order to eliminate clothes ripping at school, Brenda's instructors decide to use a negative practice procedure. Whenever Brenda attempts to rip her clothing, she will be told "No" and taken to a corner of the classroom where she will be given a sack of old clothing and rags to rip. Brenda will be told that she must rip all of the sack's contents and that she can't return to her desk until she has done so. If she won't rip them or rips too slowly, one of the instructors will actually stay with Brenda and rapidly guide her in ripping the rags. To increase the likelihood that Brenda will want to return to her desk, a DRO program will be instituted throughout the school day in which Brenda will be reinforced frequently with attention when she hasn't ripped her clothing during prespecified intervals of time. No attention will be paid to Brenda while she's engaging in the negative practice.

Brenda's behavior during the negative practice sessions suggests that she finds it aversive. For example, she attempts to run away from the instructor who takes her to the corner and she cries during the sessions. Furthermore, within a week Brenda's rate of clothes ripping has decreased from a baseline average (see Chapter 9) of 20 incidents per day to 2. Her teachers plan to continue using the negative practice until the ripping is eliminated at school, at which point they intend to suggest to Brenda's mother that she institute the negative practice procedure at home following any attempts by Brenda to rip her clothes.

Brenda's instructors were successful because they carefully designed and followed their negative practice program. In designing the program, they considered all of the following: (1) they ensured that the negative practice required a sufficient amount of physical effort to make it aversive by having Brenda rip a sack of old clothing and rags, (2) to further ensure the aversiveness of the physical effort requirement, they rapidly guided Brenda through the ripping when she refused to do so or did so too slowly, and (3) they made sure that attention, the suspected reinforcer for clothes ripping, was delivered following the absence of clothes ripping through a DRO program and that no attention was given during the negative practice. This use of attention ensured that Brenda would be motivated to stop clothes ripping during class time and that the negative practice period would be more aversive because of the opportunities for attention that Brenda was missing.

Negative practice is often confused with satiation because the inappropriate response or behavior seems also to be the reinforcer. For example, clothes ripping is a response, yet perhaps the act itself is reinforcing. The same can be said about appropriate behaviors. For example, dancing is a behavior, yet dancing is also reinforcing. The same applies to jogging, sexual behavior, singing, and other activities. The way to tell, of course, is to check whether an individual responds in order to gain access to the activity. Nevertheless, in many situations we're never quite sure whether we're dealing with the misbehavior and/or the reinforcer for that misbehavior. There are ways to distinguish between satiation and negative practice, however.

Negative practice is given following the misbehavior, and as such it is a behavioral consequence. (When defined this way, negative practice becomes a punishment procedure. See Chapter 6.) Satiation is given prior to, or independent of, the misbehavior; thus, satiation cannot be used as a consequence. Also, negative practice deals with the misbehavior or response, whereas satiation deals with the reinforcer. Thus, if you wished to treat clothes ripping with satiation, you would provide the student with the opportunity to rip a bag of rags *before* she ripped her clothing. If, on the other hand, you wished to use negative practice, you would require the student to rip a bag of rags *after* she had ripped her clothing.

The advantages of negative practice are:

1. As an aversive consequence, it can be effective in reducing an undesirable behavior.

2. Its suppressive effects may be long lasting if the negative practice sessions are sufficiently aversive.

3. It provides the instructor with control over the student's behavior during the consequence. If the instructor is guiding the student in performing the negative practice tasks, the student can be physically prevented from engaging in undesirable behaviors.

There are several disadvantages associated with negative practice:

1. There's a good chance that the student may become combative when the instructor attempts to guide her through the negative practice. If so, either the student, the instructor, or both could be injured. Thus, you must carefully consider these potential risks and take steps to minimize the possibility that someone will be injured.

2. You must ask yourself whether or not it's a good idea to allow the student to practice her misbehavior. It may well be that all you would be doing is allowing her to learn how to misbehave better. To avoid this problem, keep very complete records of the misbehavior during the first few days of the negative practice condition. If the misbehavior is not greatly reduced during this period as compared to its frequency before the procedure, terminate the negative practice procedure and institute another type of reductive or inhibitory procedure.

3. There are many undesirable behaviors for which a negative practice procedure is inappropriate because of the potential dangers associated with using the procedure. For instance, you wouldn't consider using negative practice to treat self-abusive behavior.

4. Besides the differences between negative practice and satiation that have been mentioned (that negative practice is a consequence and deals with the misbehavior, whereas satiation is not a consequence and deals with the reinforcer for the misbehavior), there remains one final and most important difference: satiation is a nonaversive procedure, since it involves reinforcers, whereas negative practice is an aversive procedure because it is an aversive consequence. As a result, in this book negative practice is considered to be a Level 2 procedure in the Least Restrictive Treatment Model. Recall that Level 2 procedures are those that contain some aversive properties or that have some potentially serious side effects associated with them, such as extinction. Negative practice should be considered to be a Level 3 procedure when the staff

member must guide the student through negative practice sessions, since there is an increased likelihood that resistance from the student will be encountered.

Great care should be exercised when you consider the use of negative practice. You can avoid the potential problems just described by following, to the letter, the Least Restrictive Treatment Model guidelines that were discussed in Chapter 1. Negative practice can be a useful way of reducing certain behaviors; but, as will be seen in the next chapters, there are some other inhibitory procedures that are applicable to a greater number of misbehaviors and that are usually much more effective.

Practice Set 3B

Answer the following questions.

1. For which of the following misbehaviors would it be reasonable to try a negative practice procedure?

Masturbating	Screaming
Self-stimulating	Hitting other students
Ruminating	Paper tearing
Spitting	Running away
Eye poking	

2. Mr. Parsons would like to try negative practice to treat his student, Jackie, who pulls up plants and grass on the school playground. What would you suggest that he do in order to use negative practice correctly?

3. Negative practice differs from satiation in at least three ways. Can you name them?

Answers are found on page 166.

THE LEAST RESTRICTIVE TREATMENT MODEL

We've now discussed five procedures that will decrease an undesirable behavior and have grouped them into three levels within the Least Restrictive Treatment Model. Level 1 procedures contain no aversive or intrusive properties, while Level 2 procedures do contain some aversive or intrusive properties. Although Level 2 procedures are not very restrictive of the student's rights, you still should obtain written approval from your administration and the student or her parents or guardian before using a Level 2 procedure. Level 3 procedures are quite aversive and intrusive. Their use requires written permission from the student or her parents, the administration, and the human rights committee.

Level 1	Level 2	Level 3
DRO (Differential Reinforcement of Other Behavior) DRA (Differential Reinforcement of Appropriate Behavior) DRI (Differential Reinforcement of Incompatible Behavior) Satiation	Negative practice (when manual guidance is not given)	Negative practice (when manual guidance is given)

SUMMARY

Satiation is a procedure in which a reinforcer that has been maintaining a misbehavior is presented noncontingently in unlimited amounts in order to reduce that behavior. When using satiation, it's necessary to always (1) make sure the reinforcer maintaining the misbehavior has been correctly identified, and (2) provide large quantities of the reinforcer before the student has a chance to misbehave. Satiation with food can be effectively used to control nonlife-threatening rumination, but records of the student's weight and the amounts of food consumed must be kept. The advantage of satiation is that it is nonaversive and nonintrusive. Its disadvantages are that (1) it rarely eliminates the misbehavior, (2) it's only temporarily effective, (3) there is a danger of reinforcing the misbehavior, and (4) there are only a few misbehaviors for which it's appropriate.

Negative practice is a procedure in which the misbehaving student is required to repeatedly practice her misbehavior. To design an effective negative practice program, it's necessary to see (1) that the practice requires enough physical effort to make it aversive, (2) that the student is guided through the practice when she tries to avoid it or does it too slowly, and (3) that the suspected reinforcer of the misbehavior is delivered during times when the misbehavior or practice are not being performed. The advantages of negative practice are that (1) it will reduce the misbehavior if the practice period is sufficiently aversive, (2) its suppressive effects may be long lasting, and (3) it provides control over the student's physical movements during the consequence. The disadvantages of negative practice include: (1) the student may become combative when required to go through negative practice, (2) it may be questionable whether a student should be allowed to practice a misbehavior, and (3) it's not an appropriate procedure for many undesirable behaviors.

Negative practice and satiation are sometimes confused, but they can be differentiated in three ways. Negative practice follows the misbehavior, making the procedure a consequence, while satiation is given independently of the misbehavior and thus can't be a consequence. Negative practice deals with the response, while satiation deals with the reinforcer. And finally, negative practice is an aversive, intrusive procedure, while satiation is not.

Since satiation is a nonaversive procedure, it is considered to be a Level 1 procedure in the Least Restrictive Treatment Model. Negative practice is considered to be a Level 2 procedure when the student performs it independently and a Level 3 procedure when the student must be manually guided through the procedure.

SUGGESTED READINGS

Ayllon, T. Intensive treatment of psychotic behavior by stimulus satiation and food reinforcement. *Behaviour Research and Therapy*, 1963, *1*, 53-61.

Barton, E. J., & Ascione, T. R. Social reinforcer satiation outcome of frequency, not ambiguity—sometimes. *Developmental Psychology*, 1978, *14*, 363-370.

Carroll, S. W., Sloop, E. W., Mutter, S., & Prince, P. L. The elimination of chronic clothes ripping in retarded people through a combination of procedures. *Mental Retardation*, 1978, *16*, 246-249.

Foxx, R. M., Snyder, M. S., & Schroeder, F. A food satiation and oral hygiene punishment program to suppress chronic rumination by retarded persons. *Journal of Autism and Developmental Disorders*, 1979, *9*, 399-412.

Jackson, G. M., Johnson, C. R., Ackron, G. S., & Crowley, R. Food satiation as a procedure to decelerate vomiting. *American Journal of Mental Deficiency*, 1975, *80*, 223-227.

Review Set 3

1. S_____ is the noncontingent presentation of large amounts of a reinforcer.

2. Satiation is always presented n_____.

3. In satiation, care must be taken so the reinforcer isn't delivered f_____ the misbehavior.

4. The advantage of satiation is that it is n_____.

5. Satiation does not e_____ a behavior, it merely reduces it.

6. The effects of satiation are t_____.

7. Satiation is effective for only a f_____ misbehaviors.

8. Requiring a student to repeatedly practice his misbehavior is called n_____ p_____.

9. N_____ p_____ follows the misbehavior, whereas s_____ is presented noncontingently.

10. The effects of negative practice can be l_____ lasting and the misbehavior may be greatly r_____.

11. Sometimes during negative practice it's necessary to p_____ guide the student in performing the repeated acts, which allows c_____ of behavior during the consequence.

12. Students may become c_____ when required to undergo negative practice.

13. Major disadvantages of negative practice are that it may allow practice of a m_____ and that it is not appropriate for many u_____ behaviors.

14. Satiation, being nonaversive, is a Level 1 procedure, while negative practice is a Level 2 procedure when performed i_____ by the student and a Level 3 procedure when m_____ g_____ must be given.

Answers are found on pages 166 and 167.

CHAPTER 4

Extinction

In the last chapter we completed the set of nonaversive procedures and were introduced to an aversive procedure, negative practice. Here we'll discuss another procedure, extinction. We'll explain how to do it and caution you about related behavioral effects that may result when it's used. The advantages and disadvantages of extinction, and its ranking in the Least Restrictive Treatment Model, will be presented as well.

> Extinction is a procedure in which the reinforcer that has been sustaining or increasing an undesirable behavior is withheld.

A behavior or response is increased and then maintained when it is followed by a positive reinforcer. However, if the reinforcer is withheld permanently, that behavior will eventually cease. When this occurs, we say that the behavior was extinguished; the procedure itself is called extinction.

Undoubtedly, extinction is the most widely used procedure for decreasing the behavior of retarded students. There are three reasons why. First, the procedure is easy to understand. All you have to do is refrain from delivering a reinforcer. In essence, you do nothing following the undesirable behavior. Second, many of the undesirable behaviors of retarded students are reinforced by attention from their instructors. Hence the use of extinction for these undesirable behaviors is simply a matter of ignoring them. Third, everyone has had a great deal of practice ignoring the undesirable behavior of others. All of us at one time or another have ignored the behavior of our children, spouses, bosses, parents, and in-laws, as well as that of salespersons, beggars, and teachers. Thus, the use of extinction comes naturally to most people. Unfortunately the use of extinction in the classroom or living unit isn't as easy as it seems, since it has many potential pitfalls. We'll discuss these potential problems later when we describe the disadvantages of extinction. However, right now, let's look at an example of the proper way to conduct an extinction program.

Bruce is a severely retarded adolescent who constantly demands attention from his instructors. In fact, he'll do just about anything to gain their attention, whether it be exposing his genitals, blowing his nose and smearing the mucus on himself, or pushing his face very close to another person and then hugging that person. His instructors have chosen to work on his exposing himself, since they're convinced that their attention has been maintaining this behavior.

During a 7-day baseline period (see Chapter 9), the instructors continue to treat Bruce's exposing himself as they have always done, by telling him to raise his pants. They find after 7 days that Bruce exposes himself about 14 times per day on the average. Having ensured that the behavior wasn't decreasing during baseline, the instructors institute an extinction program the following day. They all agree that none of them will look at or speak to Bruce when he pulls his pants down or is discovered with them down. Rather, they'll simply guide him in raising his pants without speaking or looking at him. Furthermore, they decide to give him generous amounts of attention when he's not misbehaving. To do so, they'll check him every 10 minutes. During the first day of extinction, Bruce's rate of exposing himself increases to 30 times. Bruce's exposing himself remains higher than baseline the second day, and in addition, he begins throwing tantrums and trying to attack the instructors and other students. On the third day, Bruce exposes himself 40 times and begins attempting to smear mucus on the instructors.

The instructors have not reacted to Bruce's inappropriate behaviors; rather, they've maintained impassive faces and a stony silence. Their only interactions with Bruce when he has exposed himself, other than guiding him in raising his pants, come when he attempts to attack people or wipe mucus on them. In those instances they calmly guide him away without speaking or looking at him. Over the next few days, there's a dramatic reduction in the number of times Bruce exposes himself and an equally dramatic increase in his appropriate behavior. After 2½ weeks of the extinction program, Bruce has stopped exposing himself.

The instructors' use of extinction with Bruce was correct and they were rewarded for their efforts by the elimination of Bruce's inappropriate behavior. Let's now look at why their extinction program worked. First and foremost, the instructors were consistent and persistent. All of them ignored Bruce's exposing himself as well as the other undesirable behaviors he displayed. Second, they didn't become dismayed when Bruce's exposing himself dramatically increased in frequency during the first few days of the program. Third, they provided Bruce with attention for appropriate behavior while withholding attention whenever he exposed himself. By doing so, they helped Bruce form the discrimination that attention would be forthcoming for appropriate behavior but withheld for inappropriate behavior.

To use extinction correctly and successfully, you must be prepared for the following phenomena that usually occur when a student's behavior has been placed on extinction.

The undesirable behavior gets worse before it gets better. In most cases, the frequency, severity, and/or intensity of the undesirable behavior increases during the first few days to a week that the extinction program is in effect because the student is attempting to force you to abandon the program, no doubt because such efforts have been successful in the past. The student has usually had a history of successfully forcing her instructors and parents to attend to her by becoming extremely persistent in performing the misbehavior. This is one of the major reasons it may initially seem difficult to extinguish the misbehavior.

There's a gradual reduction in the misbehavior. Usually extinction doesn't have an immediate effect on the misbehavior. The misbehavior will continue for some indeterminate period of time before it stops. The length of time required for extinction to take effect depends on (1) how many times the student received reinforcement for the misbehavior in the past, (2) whether or not every misbehavior was reinforced with attention (if the misbehavior has been reinforced continuously, it tends to extinguish fairly rapidly, whereas it usually persists if it has been reinforced intermittently), (3) the student's deprivation level, that is, how badly she wants the attention, how long she has been without it, and whether or not she has alternative sources of obtaining attention (this is why a combination of extinction with either a DRO or DRA procedure will reduce a misbehavior more rapidly than the use of either procedure alone), and (4) how much effort is required to perform the response (in general, the more effort that is required, the sooner extinction will be successful).

Extinction-induced aggression may occur. Especially during the first few days of extinction, the student may aggress against staff, her classmates, fellow residents, objects, or herself. This same phenomenon occurs when you hit or kick a vending machine that has taken your money but hasn't delivered the item you chose. In effect, the first stages of extinction are like punishment by removal or withdrawal of a positive reinforcer (see Chapters 6 and 7) in that aggressive behavior by the person under extinction or being punished is not uncommon.

Spontaneous recovery may occur. Occasionally the misbehavior will reappear after it has been extinguished or absent for a time. This phenomenon is called spontaneous recovery. You don't need to worry about it: simply ignore the misbehavior as you did before and it will quickly disappear. *Under no circumstances should you regard the extinction program as unsuccessful and thus abandon it if the behavior reappears briefly after it is extinguished.*

It only takes one person attending to the misbehavior on one occasion to wreck an extinction procedure. It can't be overemphasized that everyone in the student's environment needs to be committed to the extinction program. There are some ways of preventing uninformed individuals from inadvertently paying attention to the misbehavior. One way is to post a sign on the outside of the classroom or unit door, alerting anyone entering the room that no attention is to be given to the student unless permission to do so is given by one of the classroom instructors or staff. Or you can intercept any visitors to your classroom or living unit and explain the extinction program to them. Another way is simply to not allow visitors to enter the classroom or living unit unless they are accompanied by a staff member. All of the staff must be kept up to date about the extinction procedure. When instructors return from sick leave or vacation, for example, be sure to call and inform them about the extinction procedure before they return to work. Failure to prevent inadvertent attention will result in all your efforts at extinguishing the misbehavior going for naught. When dealing with severely and profoundly retarded students, it's usually unnecessary to ensure that a student's classmates or fellow residents won't attend to her misbehavior. However, when dealing with moderately retarded students, you must gain the cooperation of the student's classmates so that they don't reinforce her undesirable behavior with their attention. This cooperation can be gained by reinforcing them for not attending to the student's misbehavior and/or instituting a negative consequence for them if they do.

An excellent example of what happens during extinction can be found in those rare bad arguments that occur between a married couple. During the argument, the arguing behavior of both parties is reinforced by each other's verbal behavior. But what happens when one spouse becomes tired and chooses to quit arguing by merely clamming up? The other spouse, who wishes to pursue the argument, has been placed on extinction because the arguments go unanswered. What does this person on extinction typically do first? The intensity of the response is increased; the person's argumentative talk grows louder. But still there's no reinforcement because the other person doesn't respond. So what does the spouse on extinction do next? He or she introduces unrelated but troublesome issues into the argument. But still there's no response from the spouse who is tired of arguing and is not answering. Then what happens? The spouse on extinction begins to argue even more loudly and questions the other's general worth as a person. Still no response. At this point, the spouse seeking a reaction has only one alternative left: to bring up a taboo subject. Usually the taboo subject is something that the quiet spouse had confessed to previously, had been forgiven for, and had been told would never be brought up and discussed again. Or the taboo subject is an especially sensitive area related to the quiet spouse's physical appearance, success in life, or personality. And what usually happens? The angry spouse brings the taboo subject up, and the quiet spouse responds quite angrily and thereby reinforces the behavior of the angry spouse. However, if the silent spouse remains silent, there is nothing left for the angry spouse to say. He or she may throw a few dishes or call a lawyer, but the verbal behavior has been successfully extinguished.

The advantages of extinction are:

1. It may be simple, provided that all staff are consistent and persistent.
2. It will effectively eliminate a misbehavior.
3. It will produce a long-lasting effect.
4. It's a relatively nonaversive procedure. However, because it may produce aggression and emotional behavior as well as an initial increase in the intensity, severity, and frequency of the behavior being extinguished, it's classified as a Level 2 procedure in the Least Restrictive Treatment Model.

The disadvantages of extinction are:

1. The misbehavior is initially likely to increase in frequency and intensity.
2. The procedure may not be simple, since it requires incredible consistency and persistence on the part of staff members.

3. It's not rapid—the misbehavior takes time to eliminate.

4. The student may become aggressive during the initial stages of the procedure.

5. Sometimes it's difficult to determine the reinforcer that's maintaining the undesirable behavior. This is an important point since ignoring and extinction are not one and the same. It does no good to ignore a behavior that's not reinforced by attention because the behavior won't decrease. Only when the reinforcer is attention will ignoring serve in an extinction procedure as the withholding of the reinforcer.

6. The schedule of reinforcement is unknown, so you are never sure how long extinction will be necessary. For example, if an inappropriate behavior is reinforced on an average of every thirtieth response or every 8 hours, it'll take a considerable amount of time to extinguish the behavior.

7. Some misbehaviors simply can't be ignored; for example, you wouldn't use extinction to treat self-abuse, aggression towards others or objects, running away, screaming, or stripping. The use of extinction might initially increase these dangerous and/or highly disruptive behaviors or elicit aggressive responses.

In summary, the success of an extinction procedure depends on your being *consistent, patient, and persistent.* Extinction should be regarded as a Level 2 procedure in the Least Restrictive Treatment Model.

Practice Set 4

Answer the following questions.

1. For which of the following misbehaviors would it be reasonable to try an extinction procedure?

Masturbating in public   Hitting others

Self-stimulating   Out-of-seat behavior

Whining   Running away

Screaming   Throwing objects

Pestering   Cursing

2. Dick steps in front of the teacher whenever she is talking or working with another resident. How could his teacher use extinction to eliminate Dick's attention seeking?

3. Ms. Kelly has been using an extinction procedure for 2 days in an attempt to eliminate Conrad's whining. She is concerned because Conrad has been whining very loudly and aggressing

towards other students since she started the program. What would you tell her regarding her concerns?

4. You are describing the advantages of extinction to a group of staff members at a workshop. What would you tell them?

5. What disadvantages of extinction would you describe to them?

The answers are on page 167.

THE LEAST RESTRICTIVE TREATMENT MODEL

We've now discussed six procedures that will decrease an undesirable behavior and have grouped them into three levels within the Least Restrictive Treatment Model. Level 1 procedures contain no aversive or intrusive properties, while Level 2 procedures do contain some aversive or intrusive properties. Although Level 2 procedures are not very restrictive of the student's rights, you still should obtain written approval from your administration and the student or her parents or guardian before using a Level 2 procedure. Level 3 procedures are quite aversive and intrusive. Their use requires written permission from the student or her parents, the administration, and the human rights committee.

Level 1	Level 2	Level 3
DRO (Differential Reinforcement of Other Behavior)	Negative practice (when manual guidance is not given)	Negative practice (when manual guidance is given)
DRA (Differential Reinforcement of Appropriate Behavior)	Extinction	
DRI (Differential Reinforcement of Incompatible Behavior)		
Satiation		

SUMMARY

Extinction is the withholding of the reinforcer that has been maintaining or increasing an undesirable behavior. There are some common phenomena associated with the use of extinction: (1) the behavior gets worse before it gets better, (2) the behavior is reduced gradually, (3) extinction-induced aggression may result, (4) spontaneous recovery may occur, and (5) the procedure is easily rendered ineffective if one person in the student's environment doesn't follow the extinction program. The advantages of extinction are that (1) it's easy to understand, (2) it eliminates the misbehavior, (3) it produces a long-lasting effect, and (4) it's relatively nonaversive. The disadvantages are that (1) the behavior initially increases in intensity and frequency, (2) the program requires incredible consistency, (3) the results are not rapid, (4) the student may become aggressive, (5) it may be difficult to determine what reinforcer is maintaining the undesirable behavior, (6) the schedule of reinforcement is unknown, and (7) some behaviors can't be ignored. Extinction is a Level 2 procedure.

SUGGESTED READINGS

Lovaas, O. I., & Simmons, J. G. Manipulation of self-destruction in three retarded children. *Journal of Applied Behavior Analysis*, 1969, *2*, 143-157.

Martin, P. L., & Foxx, R. M. Victim control of the aggression of an institutionalized retardate. *Journal of Behavior Therapy and Experimental Psychiatry*, 1973, *4*, 161-165.

Myers, D. V. Extinction, DRO, and response-cost procedures for eliminating self-injurious behavior: A case study. *Behaviour Research and Therapy*, 1975, *13*, 189-192.

Williams, C. D. The elimination of tantrum behavior by extinction procedures. *Journal of Abnormal and Social Psychology*, 1959, *59*, 269.

Review Set 4

1. E_____ is the withholding of a reinforcer.

2. Some characteristics of extinction are that (1) the behavior gets w_____ before it gets b_____, (2) the misbehavior is reduced g_____, (3) extinction-induced a_____ may occur, and (4) s_____ r_____ may occur.

3. Extinction will eventually e_____ a misbehavior and produce a l_____-lasting effect.

4. Because it only entails ignoring a response, extinction seems s_____; however, it requires an incredible amount of c_____ to be successful.

5. Although extinction is a n_____ procedure, it is ranked as a Level _____ procedure because it may produce aggression and emotional behavior and the misbehavior may initially increase.

Answers are found on page 167.

CHAPTER 5

Physical Restraint

We now move from Level 2 procedures such as extinction to a more intrusive and aversive Level 3 procedure, physical restraint. Two types of restraint, behavioral and custodial, will be defined and contrasted, and the use of manual and mechanical behavioral physical restraint will be explained. The good and bad points of physical restraint also will be mentioned, and cautions for its safe and legal use will be given.

TYPES OF PHYSICAL RESTRAINT

Physical restraint is an aversive procedure that's used almost exclusively to treat severe cases of self-abusive behavior, and occasionally to treat dangerous or highly disruptive behavior, such as severe cases of aggression towards others or property. There are two types of physical restraint—behavioral physical restraint and custodial physical restraint—and it's important from the outset that a clear distinction be made between them.

> Behavioral physical restraint is a procedure in which the student is prevented from moving his limbs and/or body for a prespecified period following the performance of a misbehavior.

Behavioral physical restraint is used as a negative consequence to follow an undesirable behavior. The duration of behavioral physical restraint is prespecified; the exact amount of time the student is to be restrained is determined before the procedure is implemented. Behavioral physical restraint is brief and usually lasts no more than 30 minutes.

> Custodial physical restraint is a procedure in which the student is noncontingently prevented from moving his limbs and/or body for an unspecified period.

Custodial restraint, on the other hand, is typically not used as a consequence. Rather, it's often applied noncontingently and arbitrarily. The duration of custodial physical restraint is rarely specified and it can often last indefinitely. There are two types of custodial physical restraint. One type is used in institutions to subdue agitated residents. It's ordered by a physician and usually consists of tying or strapping the agitated person to his bed in a spread-eagle fashion. An intramuscular injection of a tranquilizer often accompanies the restraint. The restraint usually remains in force until canceled by the physician, which means the individual can remain in restraint long after his agitation has subsided.

The other type of custodial restraint involves the use of restraint to prevent self-abuse, either in the institution or classroom. This restraint may take many forms depending on the type of self-abuse. For example, a head banger may wear a football helmet that's locked so that it can't be removed. Or an individual who smashes his face with his fists may be outfitted with arm splints that prevent him from bending his arms so that he can't hit his face. Such self-abusive individuals often wear their restraints day and night. Although these forms of custodial restraint prevent self-abuse from occurring, they do present several problems. First, the restraint may prevent the individual from participating in a variety of educational activities; for instance, the number of activities available to someone in arm splints is severely limited. Second, the restraints may cause muscle deterioration or atrophy if they've been worn for long periods of time. Third, if the person struggles against the restraints, he is in effect performing a series of isometric exercises that will only serve to make him stronger and more difficult to manage. Fourth, for some self-abusive retarded persons, the restraints themselves become reinforcing over time. If this happens, you're faced with the difficult problem of eliminating the person's reliance on the restraints. What follows is the classic Catch-22 situation. If you remove the restraints, the person hits himself; if you leave the restraints on, he doesn't hit himself. Yet he continues to suffer the physical problems and restriction from educational and programmatic activities previously described.

To summarize, here are the important distinctions between custodial physical restraint and behavioral physical restraint.

Custodial restraint is often applied noncontingently and arbitrarily and serves a purely custodial function; behavioral restraint is contingent on behavior and is prespecified, and is a programmatic intervention that includes the collection of treatment data. Behavioral physical restraint thus fits the definition of punishment (see Chapter 6) in that its use as a consequence is designed to reduce the occurrence of the misbehavior. Custodial restraint, on the other hand, generally has no impact on the future occurrence of the behavior. As a result, it's strongly recommended that custodial restraint not be used except in dire emergencies or circumstances.

USE OF BEHAVIORAL PHYSICAL RESTRAINT

There are two ways of implementing behavioral physical restraint. You can manually restrain the student with your hands and body or use some type of mechanical restraint for a prespecified period of time. Mechanical restraints include straps, auto seat belts, football helmets, and equipment especially designed for particular body parts. The following example illustrates the use of behavioral physical restraint when the instructor uses her hands to restrain a student.

Ms. Hodos has decided to use a physical restraint procedure to decrease Robby's self-abuse. Following a brief period of baseline recording (see Chapter 9), she is ready to implement the procedure. Whenever Robby hits himself, or attempts to hit himself, Ms. Hodos says, "No, don't hit yourself" and immediately restrains his hands with her hands. She stands behind Robby while he's seated at his desk so that she can hold his arms to his sides. She does not look at him or say anything. Although Robby struggles somewhat, Ms. Hodos continues to hold his hands with sufficient force to prevent him from self-abusing. The program plan calls for her to restrain Robby for 5 minutes. She releases him at the end of that time because he is not struggling. (Had he been struggling at the end of the 5-minute interval, she would have continued to restrain him until he had ceased struggling. In this way, Robby would learn that release from restraint was contingent on his being relaxed.) As she releases his arms, she says, "Don't hit yourself." She then attempts to involve him in sorting different colors of socks and reinforces him with a piece of potato stick when he touches a sock. Over time the combination of 5 minutes of physical restraint for self-abuse plus reinforcement for appropriate behavior decreases Robby's self-abuse to the point where he can sit in class all day without hitting himself.

Robby's struggling during the physical restraint suggested that it was aversive to him. However, it also could have been that he found the struggling to be exciting or reinforcing. This would have been the case if the physical restraint procedure hadn't reduced his self-abuse over time. To solve the problem of the reinforcing aspects of physical touch and/or struggling, you should consider (1) increasing the duration of physical restraint, (2) using wrestling and physical touch as a reinforcer for appropriate behavior, or (3) using mechanical restraint devices. This next example illustrates the use of behavioral physical restraint when the instructor uses a mechanical device.

Ms. Hodos has decided to treat Robby's self-abuse by employing a physical restraint procedure that involves the contingent application of mechanical restraints. Whenever Robby hits himself, she says, "No, don't hit yourself" and immediately slips a splint-like device over each of his arms. Robby is required to wear the restraints for 5 minutes, after which they are removed. While he's wearing them, Ms. Hodos does not look at him or say anything. When he's not restrained, Ms. Hodos or her aide provides Robby with reinforcers for engaging in appropriate behaviors that involve his hands. Ms. Hodos is confident that the arm splints will reduce Robby's self-abuse because he often cries and becomes agitated when he is required to wear them. Her observations are ultimately confirmed, because within 2 weeks, Robby's self-abuse is eliminated in the classroom.

The success of these two behavioral physical restraint procedures was a direct result of Ms. Hodos' consistent use of the procedures in combination with a DRI procedure. Furthermore, Ms. Hodos made every effort to minimize the attention associated with the use of physical restraint.

There are several advantages associated with the use of behavioral physical restraint:

1. The major advantage is that the misbehavior can't occur during the procedure. Thus, physical restraint procedures produce immediate and complete suppression of the misbehavior so long as they are in force.
2. The misbehavior may be eliminated, that is, reduced to zero.
3. The procedure may have long-lasting effects, so that the misbehavior remains at zero.

The latter two advantages are the result of the aversive nature of behavioral physical restraint procedures.

There are several disadvantages associated with the use of behavioral physical restraint:

1. The procedure can be highly aversive and intrusive, so great care and judgment must be exercised when it's used.

2. The restraint can become reinforcing if a lot of attention is associated with the implementation of the procedure. Many retarded persons, especially if they are profoundly or severely retarded, find being touched to be a powerful reinforcer, especially if the majority of their physical interactions with people are limited to being touched during a restraint procedure. To minimize this possibility, you should use physical contact, such as a hug, touch, or caress, as a reinforcer for appropriate behavior. Some students even find mechanical restraints to be reinforcing if their use represents the major source of attention that they receive. Such an iatrogenic effect (a medical term meaning the treatment causes as bad or worse problems than the problem that's being treated) usually results from the long-term use of mechanical restraint in a custodial, rather than a behavioral, fashion. In such situations, your use of behavioral physical restraint may be counterproductive to the successful elimination of the student's misbehavior. You can usually identify such students because they'll self-restrain in their own clothing if denied access to the mechanical restraints or attempt to grab your hands or arms. For these students it's best to use some other type of reductive procedure.

3. The student's struggling during the restraint can constitute a period of isometric exercise. When this occurs, we are presented with another iatrogenic effect, namely, that the use of the restraint procedure creates a stronger student who is thereby able to better resist the restraint procedure. This is more likely to occur when mechanical (rather than manual) restraint is used, since the amount of restraint required cannot be adjusted according to the student's struggling. Furthermore, the student doesn't learn that relaxing leads to a reduction in the amount of restraint. These problems are overcome by using manual restraint, since you can adjust the amount of restraint given from moment to moment, depending on how much the student is struggling. In this way the student learns to relax during the procedure. However, despite the obvious advantage of using manual rather than mechanical restraint, there are disadvantages to the use of

manual restraint. One is that there is an increased chance that someone will be injured, since you run this risk anytime you physically intervene with a student. A second is that manual restraint is not appropriate for students who are stronger than the staff member.

4. There's the danger that the procedure could be used in an arbitrary and punitive fashion. For example, a bothersome student could be placed in mechanical restraints simply as a method of getting him out of the instructor's way. This is usually not a problem if the instructor uses her hands to apply the physical restraint, since she is required to interact with the student in an effortful way.

5. The procedure requires the full participation of a staff person when the physical restraint is not mechanical. This can be a problem when there are not enough instructional staff to provide one-to-one attention to a misbehaving student.

6. There is a distinct possibility that someone may be injured because of the procedure's physically intrusive nature. The student may become combative when you attempt to implement the restraint, which can greatly increase the likelihood that one of you will be injured. Thus, it should come as no surprise that the use of physical restraint with large, aggressive students is not advocated. A more reasonable procedure to try for such students would be a timeout room (described in Chapter 7).

In summary, you should never consider using a physical restraint procedure unless the misbehavior is serious enough to warrant accepting the potential dangers associated with the use of restraint. Above all, *document what you are doing and obtain written permission from all relevant parties*—parents, the student, administrators, and human rights and/or restrictive procedures committees—before you undertake a physical restraint procedure. Finally, *make sure that all staff members who will be using the procedure have been fully trained in using it*. The best way to do this is for them to practice restraining each other under the watchful eye of the professional in charge of implementing the program. Physical restraint should never be used with a student until staff members have used it on themselves.

Practice Set 5

Answer the following questions.

1. For which of the following misbehaviors would it be reasonable to try a physical restraint procedure?

Masturbating in public   Face scratching
Rectal digging   Clothes ripping
Running away   Screaming
Throwing objects   Out-of-seat behavior
Hitting others   Pestering

2. What are three ways in which custodial physical restraint and behavioral physical restraint differ?
3. Laura hits her ears with her fists. How could her teacher use his hands to implement a behavioral physical restraint procedure to treat Laura's self-abuse?
4. How could Laura's teacher use a mechanical device to treat her self-abuse by behavioral physical restraint?
5. Why is it so important to reinforce an appropriate behavior with physical contact when using a physical restraint procedure to treat a misbehavior?

Answers are found on page 168.

THE LEAST RESTRICTIVE TREATMENT MODEL

We've now discussed seven procedures that will decrease an undesirable behavior and have grouped them into three levels within the Least Restrictive Treatment Model. Level 1 procedures contain no aversive or intrusive properties, while Level 2 procedures do contain some aversive or intrusive properties. Although Level 2 procedures are not very restrictive of the student's rights, you still should obtain written approval from your administration and the student or his parents or guardian before using a Level 2 procedure. Level 3 procedures are quite aversive and intrusive. Their use requires written permission from the student or his parents, the administration, and the human rights committee.

Level 1	Level 2	Level 3
DRO (Differential Reinforcement of Other Behavior)	Negative practice (when manual guidance is not given)	Negative practice (when manual guidance is given)
DRA (Differential Reinforcement of Appropriate Behavior)	Extinction	Physical restraint

Level 1	Level 2	Level 3
DRI (Differential Reinforcement of Incompatible Behavior) Satiation		

SUMMARY

There are two types of physical restraint, behavioral and custodial. Behavioral physical restraint is a procedure in which the student is prevented from moving his limbs and/or body for a prespecified period following the performance of a misbehavior. It's used as a negative consequence in a behavioral program, and it usually lasts for only a brief period of time. Custodial physical restraint is a procedure in which the student is noncontingently prevented from moving his limbs and/or body for an unspecified period. It's not a consequence, is used for custodial purposes only, and may last for an indefinite period of time. The main uses for custodial restraint are subduing agitated persons and stopping self-abuse. However, it creates problems when used over a long term to control self-abuse, since it (1) prevents participation in many activities, (2) may cause muscle atrophy, (3) may allow isometric strengthening of muscles, and (4) may actually become reinforcing to the student.

Behavioral physical restraint can be done manually or mechanically. When manual restraint is chosen, steps should be taken to ensure that the touching and/or struggling involved don't become reinforcing, by (1) increasing the duration of physical restraint, (2) using touch as a reinforcer for appropriate behavior, or (3) using mechanical restraints.

Advantages of behavioral physical restraint include the following: (1) the misbehavior can't occur during the procedure, (2) the misbehavior may be eliminated, and (3) the effects of the procedure may be long lasting. The disadvantages are (1) the procedure can be highly aversive and intrusive, (2) the restraint can become reinforcing, (3) mechanical restraint can cause the student to isometrically strengthen his muscles, (4) mechanical restraint can be used arbitrarily, (5) manual restraint requires full participation of a staff member, and (6) the student or staff member may be injured during the initial application of restraint.

When using physical restraint, it's necessary to document what is being done and to obtain written permission from all relevant parties, since it is a Level 3 procedure. All staff members who are going to use the procedure should be fully trained in its use.

SUGGESTED READINGS

Bitgood, S. C., Crowe, M. J., Suarez, Y., & Peters, R. O. Immobilization: Effects and side effects on stereotyped behavior in children. *Behavior Modification*, 1980, *4*, 187-208.

Bucher, B., Reykdal, B., & Albin, J. Brief physical restraint to control pica in retarded children. *Journal of Behavior Therapy and Experimental Psychiatry*, 1976, *7*, 137-140.

Favell, J. E., McGimsey, J. F., & Jones, M. L. The use of physical restraint in the treatment of self-injury and as positive reinforcement. *Journal of Applied Behavior Analysis*, 1978, *11*, 225-241.

Hamilton, J., Stephens, L., & Allen, P. Controlling aggressive and destructive behavior in severely retarded institutionalized residents. *American Journal of Mental Deficiency*, 1967, *71*, 852-856.

Henriksen, K., & Doughty, R. Decelerating undesirable mealtime behavior in a group of profoundly retarded boys. *American Journal of Mental Deficiency*, 1967, *72*, 40-44.

Review Set 5

1. P_____ r_____ is a procedure in which the student is prevented from moving his limbs and/or body.

2. Physical restraint is used almost exclusively to treat severe cases of s_____-a_____ behavior.

3. B_____ physical restraint is a behavioral consequence, whereas c_____ physical restraint is not, since it's often applied noncontingently and arbitrarily.

4. Behavioral physical restraint can be employed either m_____ or m_____.

5. To keep manual physical restraint from becoming reinforcing, you can (a) i_____ the duration of the restraint, (b) use t_____ as a reinforcer for appropriate behavior, and (c) use m_____ restraints.

6. The advantages of physical restraint are that (a) the misbehavior c_____ occur, (b) the misbehavior may be e_____, and (c) the procedure may have l_____-lasting effects.

7. The disadvantages of physical restraint are: (a) it's
   a_____ and intrusive, (b) the restraint can become
   r_____, (c) the student's struggling during restraint
   can be a form of isometric e_____, (d) mechanical
   restraint may be used in an arbitrary or p_____
   fashion, (e) the full participation of a s_____ person is
   required when the restraint is not mechanical, and (f) it is
   p_____ intrusive, thereby increasing the chance that
   someone may be injured.

8. Since physical restraint is a Level 3 procedure, it's necessary
   to d_____ what is done and obtain p_____ from
   all involved parties.

9. All staff members who use physical restraint should be
   t_____ in its use.

The answers are on page 168.

CHAPTER 6

Punishment: An Overview

With the discussion of physical restraint in the last chapter, we've begun consideration of very aversive and intrusive procedures. We'll now continue with punishment, the topic of this chapter. Here we'll provide an overview of punishment's effects and uses before discussing more specific procedures. The definition of punishment is as follows:

> Punishment is a procedure that decreases the future probability of the behavior it follows.

After we describe the two forms of punishment, we'll discuss how to tell when a consequence is a punisher and what variables influence punishment's effectiveness. The advantages and disadvantages of punishment will be listed, and two methods to increase the success of a punishment procedure will be discussed.

TYPES OF PUNISHMENT

There are two types of punishment, Type I and Type II.

> Type I punishment is the application of an aversive event following a misbehavior.

This type of punishment involves the application of an aversive event following the misbehavior that reduces the future performance of that behavior. Some examples of these aversive events include spanking, shaking, and shouting at someone. Type I punishment is typically used in situations and environments where the person implementing the punishment procedure has almost com-

61

plete control over the person being punished. Thus, it's not surprising that this type of punishment is most commonly used by parents, in the military, and in prisons. However, as you'll learn later, certain humane and ethically defensible forms of Type I punishment can be used with developmentally disabled persons.

> Type II punishment is the withdrawal of a positive
> reinforcer following a misbehavior.

This type of punishment involves the withdrawal of a positive reinforcer following the misbehavior that reduces the future performance of that behavior. Examples of this type of punishment include social disapproval (withdrawing your attention from the student), fines, timeout, and penalties. The most pervasive form used with retarded students is timeout from positive reinforcement, which will be discussed in the next chapter. In general, Type II punishment is more widely used with retarded individuals than Type I.

DETERMINATION OF WHETHER
A CONSEQUENCE IS PUNISHING

We've all encountered students or individuals who don't seem to be affected by what we would consider to be punishing consequences. For instance, there's general agreement that being scolded is a punishing or aversive experience, yet the behavior of some children remains unaffected when their parents scold them. In this case scolding is obviously not a punishing consequence and in fact might even be maintaining (reinforcing) the misbehavior. An even more extreme example is masochism. Someone who is excited by a certain type of pain hardly finds that pain to be a punishing experience. The point is, it's very unwise to make sweeping generalizations about what is punishing for someone (or, for that matter, reinforcing). This is why you should always *specify or define a consequence by its effect on the behavior.* If it increases the behavior, it's a reinforcing consequence; if it decreases the behavior, it's a punishing consequence. Thus, we should attend to how a consequence affects the behavior rather than to the nature of the consequence itself. The following example illustrates this point.

A kiss, hug, or extra piece of pie can under certain conditions function as punishers (events that reduce the behavior they follow). Imagine you are sitting next to a person who is writing on a note pad. If you were to kiss her every time her pen touched the writing pad, one of two things would probably happen. If she found your kisses reinforcing, her rate of note writing in your presence would increase. If she found your kisses offensive, her rate of writing notes in your presence would decrease markedly. In this latter instance, your kiss by definition would be a punisher. Similarly, a hug from you, if it were offensive to her, would decrease her note taking. Or if she had just finished a large lunch and was full, force-feeding her bits of her favorite food, say apple pie, each time she wrote on the pad would decrease her note taking. Thus, under certain circumstances events we ordinarily regard as powerful reinforcers can serve as punishers, and vice versa. This should clarify that when we speak of punishing a behavior, we're discussing the use of an ethically defensible behavioral event that will decrease that behavior, not some barbaric procedure designed to cause physical or psychological harm or distress.

VARIABLES INFLUENCING THE EFFECTIVENESS OF PUNISHMENT

There are several variables that influence whether or not a punishment procedure will be effective. One is whether or not the punishment is implemented immediately. The sooner the punishment follows the misbehavior, the more likely it is that it will effectively reduce the misbehavior. The importance of immediacy cannot be overstressed, especially when you're dealing with profoundly and severely retarded students who don't mediate time spans very well. The most humane way of using punishment with these students is to use it immediately following the misbehavior so they can associate their misbehavior with the receipt of punishment.

A second variable is the intensity of the punishment. As a rule, the more intense the punishment, the more effective it will be in suppressing the unwanted behavior. Obviously this variable should be considered when selecting a punishment procedure but should not be the determining factor in that selection.

A third variable is the schedule of punishment, that is, whether or not the punishment is delivered each time the misbehavior occurs. To maximize the effectiveness of a punishment procedure, it should follow *each* occurrence of the undesirable behavior. Otherwise the behavior being punished is on an intermittent schedule of punishment, which means, in effect, that it's also being strengthened through intermittent reinforcement.

The final and most important variable is whether or not an alternative behavior will be reinforced. The cardinal rule in using punishment is *always provide reinforcement for an alternative appropriate behavior.* If attention is suspected to be the reinforcer that is maintaining the misbehavior, provide attention for an appropriate behavior and punishment for the misbehavior. In addition to making your punishment procedure work effectively, the reinforcement of an alternative behavior offers another benefit; namely, it won't be necessary to use an extremely intense punishment procedure. Scientific research has shown that mild forms of punishment are highly effective when the student has some means of obtaining reinforcement other than by the misbehavior that's being punished.

To summarize, by carefully considering these four variables when you design a punishment procedure, you'll be treating the misbehaving student in a humane fashion. When you maximize the effectiveness of a punishment procedure, it works more quickly, thus reducing the number of times the punishment is necessary.

Practice Set 6A

Answer the following questions.

1. After Marilyn bit her little sister, Marilyn's mother spanked her. Marilyn's mother used what type of punishment?

2. After Alice broke her mother's vase, her mother sent Alice to her room for 30 minutes. What type of punishment did Alice's mother use?

3. Ms. Ryan has been requiring Robert to sit in the corner for 5 minutes whenever he hits one of the other residents. She sends him to the corner because she thinks it's punishing, but there's been no decrease in Robert's hitting in the 2 weeks since she has been using the procedure. What has Ms. Ryan learned about this supposed punishing consequence?

4. Mr. Jefferson, Jonathan's teacher, has instituted a punishment program to reduce Jonathan's screaming in class. As part of his program he intends to liberally reinforce Jonathan for on-task behavior. Mr. Jefferson is following the cardinal rule for using punishment. What is it?

5. You are describing the four variables that influence the effectiveness of a punishment procedure to some of your fellow aides. What would you tell them?

Answers are found on pages 168 and 169.

ADVANTAGES AND DISADVANTAGES OF PUNISHMENT

There are several advantages of using punishment to decrease a behavior:

1. Punishment can immediately suppress the behavior when applied correctly.

2. It may produce a long-lasting effect. The future probability of the misbehavior's occurrence is greatly reduced when punishment is used effectively.

3. Punishment may produce complete suppression of the misbehavior, that is, reduce it to zero.

4. It may affect the behavior of the misbehaving student's classmates or fellow residents, since its use reduces the chance that others will imitate the misbehavior. Having observed the punishing consequence being applied, other students may be less likely to misbehave since they won't want to receive the punishment.

5. It may produce an irreversible suppression effect. When punishment is used maximally, the behavior may be eliminated forever in those situations in which it was punished. For example, people normally only put their fingers in a light socket once. Once shocked, they don't test other light sockets. This advantage distinguishes punishment from any other reductive procedure because no procedure, other than punishment, can produce an irreversible effect. However, it's highly unlikely that you will ever use a punishment procedure of sufficient intensity to obtain the irreversible effect. That's why we must typically program the punishment procedure across all settings and situations.

Punishment is not a panacea; it has several disadvantages or negative side effects. The disadvantages of punishment are:

1. Punishment may produce emotional behavior. The student may become nervous and upset when she is about to be or is punished.

2. The punished student may become aggressive when she is punished. This aggression can either be elicited or operant. In elicited aggression, the student attacks anyone or anything nearby, say a classmate or an inanimate object. The aggression is said to be elicited because it isn't directed toward the source of the punishment (the instructor). In operant aggression, the punished student attacks the source of the punishment, her instructor, in an attempt to end the punishment.

3. Negative modeling may occur. When you punish a student, you run the risk of teaching her how to punish others. In negative modeling you serve as a model for the student to imitate, and in this case, you are modeling how to punish others. Negative modeling offers one explanation for why children who were abused by their parents tend to grow up to become child abusers.

4. The student may attempt to escape or avoid the punishing situation or person. This is a very serious disadvantage because your opportunities to have positive interactions with the student are severely limited if she avoids interacting with you or attempts to escape interactions.

Fortunately there's a very simple way of avoiding or reducing the possibility that these disadvantages or side effects will occur. Follow the cardinal rule when using punishment: *always reinforce an alternative appropriate response.* By doing so, you'll reduce the student's anxiety, the possibility that she will attack you or someone else, and her desire to avoid or escape interacting with you. You'll also be helping the student to form the discrimination that appropriate behavior will be reinforced while inappropriate behavior will be punished. And you'll be serving as a more positive model since you'll be modeling how to reinforce others.

CONDITIONED AVERSIVE STIMULI

A conditioned aversive stimulus is a neutral stimulus that has acquired its aversive or punishing properties from being repeatedly paired with a punishing event.

When using a punishment procedure, your ultimate goal is to reduce and eventually eliminate its use. In order to do this, you should always pair a conditioned aversive stimulus with the punishing event.

The word *no*, frowns, and negative gestures such as shaking your fist at someone may become conditioned aversive stimuli. We regard these events as aversive because they have been paired in the past with punishing events, such as spankings, scoldings, and even physical attacks. The word *no* itself had no meaning for us until it was paired with these punishing events. Eventually, however, *no* came to mean that we were to stop what we were doing or that we were being instructed not to do something. It's very important for you to always pair the word *no* with the delivery of punishment. By doing so, the word *no* may eventually suppress the student's misbehavior. The use of *no* as a conditioned aversive stimulus is crucial because it offers you a simple way of controlling the student's misbehavior without having to resort to the full punishment procedure each time. Furthermore, it's a more normal way of discouraging someone from misbehaving.

PUNISHMENT AND BEHAVIOR CHAINS

Rarely does our behavior, whether appropriate or inappropriate, consist simply of a single response followed by a reinforcer. Rather, we typically engage in a series or sequence of responses, a *behavior chain*, that results in some important reinforcer at the end of the sequence. Because the reinforcer comes at the end of the sequence, it's called a *terminal reinforcer* (SR^+). Examples of behavior chains that you perform include shopping, bathing, going out for the evening, driving to work, and bowling.

> A behavior (stimulus-response) chain is a sequence
> of stimuli and responses that ends with a terminal
> reinforcer.

We perform these long sequences (chains) of behavior even though the reinforcer only appears at the end of the behavior chain. We do so because of conditioned reinforcement. Each response in the chain is followed by an event (a stimulus) that reinforces that response (conditioned reinforcement) while simultaneously serving as a discriminative stimulus for the next response. A discriminative stimulus is also a conditioned reinforcer (S^{r+}) because it has been associated or paired with reinforcement. Thus, a stimulus in a behavior chain serves a dual role as a conditioned reinforcer (S^{r+}) for the response (R) it follows and a discriminative stimulus (S^D) for the response it precedes. In its role as a conditioned reinforcer, the stimulus maintains and strengthens the response it follows; in its role as a discriminative stimulus, it ensures that the next response in the chain will occur. Let's look at a common behavior—eating at a fast-food restaurant —as a stimulus-response (S-R) chain.

(1) $S^D \rightarrow$ (restaurant sign)   (2) $R \rightarrow$ (drive into parking lot)   (3) $S^D \rightarrow$ (door of restaurant)   (4) $R \rightarrow$ (enter restaurant)

(5) $S^D \rightarrow$ (6) $R \rightarrow$ (7) $S^D \rightarrow$ (8) $R \rightarrow$
(counter)   (walk to   (menu on   (read menu)
            counter)   wall)

(9) $S^D \rightarrow$ (10) $R \rightarrow$ (11) $S^D \rightarrow$ (12) $R \rightarrow$
(counter   (order   (food on   (pay
employee)   food)   tray)   counter
("May I take   ("That will   employee)
your   be $1.98,
order?")   please.")

(13) $S^D \rightarrow$ (14) $R \rightarrow$ (15) $S^D \rightarrow$ (16) $R \rightarrow$
(food on   (carry food   (food on   (eat)
tray)   to table)   table)

S^{R+}
(delicious
food)

As the example shows, the promise of delicious food at the end of the chain is sufficient to produce a number of responses and these responses are reinforced by the discriminative stimuli that follow each of them along the way.

In any stimulus-response or behavior chain the last response in the chain is the strongest because it's always associated with the immediate delivery of the terminal reinforcer. (The terminal reinforcer is always a more powerful reinforcer than any of the conditioned reinforcers, the discriminative stimuli, that are a part of the behavioral chain.) Conversely, the first response is the weakest response because it's furthest away from the terminal reinforcer. Thus, if you wish to use punishment to weaken a maladaptive behavior chain, you should punish a response that occurs very early in the chain. By doing so, you'll be maximizing the effectiveness of the punisher because a weak response is likely to be suppressed quickly, whereas a response close to the terminal reinforcer will be more difficult to suppress because of its close association with that reinforcer. Also, punishing a response early in the chain disrupts the chain, thereby preventing the effects of the rest of the behavior chain. For example, consider the differences in outcome between punishing self-abusive head banging as the student moves her head toward a concrete wall versus after her head has hit the wall.

Here's an example of how a knowledge of stimulus-response chains can be used to design an effective punishment program. After Stewart has hit someone, he tells his teacher what he's done.

His teacher then admonishes him and tells him not to hit others. Stewart listens intently, but there's been no decrease in his hitting. It's apparent that Stewart enjoys the negative attention he receives from the teacher and that this attention is probably the terminal reinforcer in Stewart's aggressive behavior chain.

Stewart's aggressive behavior chain could consist of several behaviors or responses that end with his hitting someone. In fact, Stewart's teacher identified the following behavior chain after she had observed him closely for a couple of days.

(1) $S^D \longrightarrow$ (Teacher talking to another student)	(2) $R \longrightarrow$ (Stewart walks toward Ethel)	(3) $S^D \longrightarrow$ (Ethel rocking in a corner)	(4) $R \longrightarrow$ (Stewart begins to mutter)
(5) $S^D \longrightarrow$ (Ethel ignoring Stewart)	(6) $R \longrightarrow$ (Stewart steps closer and touches Ethel)	(7) $S^D \longrightarrow$ (Teacher telling Stewart to leave Ethel alone)	(8) $R \longrightarrow$ (Stewart looks at Teacher and steps closer)
(9) $S^D \longrightarrow$ (Ethel's head)	(10) $R \longrightarrow$ (Stewart hits Ethel's head)	(11) $S^D \longrightarrow$ (Teacher running over to Ethel)	(12) $R \longrightarrow$ (Stewart tells Teacher he hit Ethel)

S^{R+}
(Teacher telling
Stewart he
was
inappropriate)

Having made this analysis of Stewart's aggressive behavior chain, his teacher decided to punish him whenever he stood by another student and muttered, since that behavior always preceded his hitting someone.

Therefore, to maximize the punishment process, always punish early in the maladaptive behavior chain. You might think that this is unfair, since the student hasn't yet performed the misbehavior. However, punishing early in the chain is actually more humane. By doing so, it won't be necessary to use punishment as many times as would be required if the punishment followed the misbehavior.

Practice Set 6B

1. Name the five advantages of punishment.
2. Name the four disadvantages of punishment.
3. On one occasion Elliot tried to hit Ms. Ryan when she sent him to the corner. On another occasion he kicked the trash can on his way to the corner. Elliot's attack towards Ms. Ryan represented what kind of aggression? His kicking the trash can represented what kind of aggression?
4. Ms. Connors said, "No, Rose, don't pick your nose!" Ms. Connors was using the word *no* as what?
5. Avner always bangs the table with his fists before he runs out of the room. When should Avner's behavior chain of running away be punished? Why?

Answers are found on page 169.

SUMMARY

Punishment is a procedure that decreases the future frequency of the behavior it follows. There are two types of punishment: Type I punishment is the application of an aversive event following a misbehavior; Type II punishment is the withdrawal of a positive reinforcer following a misbehavior. It can't be said that a consequence is punishing or reinforcing until its effect on the behavior it follows is seen. If the behavior increases, the consequence is reinforcing; if the behavior decreases, the consequence is punishing. Several variables influence the effectiveness of punishment: (1) the immediacy with which the punishment is delivered, (2) the intensity of the punishment, (3) the schedule of punishment, and (4) whether or not an alternative appropriate behavior is being reinforced.

The advantages of using punishment are that it (1) can immediately suppress the misbehavior, (2) may produce a long-lasting effect, (3) may eliminate the misbehavior, (4) may prevent others from performing the same misbehavior, and (5) may produce irreversible suppression of the misbehavior. However, there are disadvantages as well: (1) punishment may produce emotional behavior, (2) the punished student may display elicited or operant aggression, (3) negative modeling may occur, and (4) the student may attempt to escape or avoid punishing situations or people. These disadvantages can be reduced by following the cardinal rule of always reinforcing an alternative appropriate response when using punishment procedures.

Punishment procedures should be designed to be reduced and eliminated as soon as possible. One way is by pairing a conditioned aversive stimulus with the punishing event. A conditioned aversive stimulus is a neutral stimulus that has acquired aversive properties because it has been repeatedly paired with a punishing event. A classic example of a conditioned aversive stimulus is the word *no*. With time the conditioned aversive stimulus alone may be sufficient to suppress the misbehavior. Also, punishment should always be applied as early as possible in the behavior chain that leads to a misbehavior. A behavior chain is a sequence of stimuli and responses that ends with a terminal reinforcer. Because the strongest behaviors are those closest to the terminal reinforcer, it's easier to suppress the earlier behaviors in the chain. This also prevents the remainder of the chain from occurring.

SUGGESTED READINGS

Azrin, N. H., & Holz, W. C. Punishment. In W. K. Honig (Ed.), *Operant behavior.* New York: Appleton-Century-Crofts, 1966.

Catania, A. C. *Learning.* Englewood Cliffs, N.J.: Prentice-Hall, 1979.

Gardner, W. I. Use of punishment procedures with the severely retarded. *American Journal of Mental Deficiency,* 1969, *74*, 86-103.

Harris, S. L., & Ersner-Hershfield, R. Behavioral suppression of seriously disruptive behavior in psychotic and retarded patients: A review of punishment and its alternatives. *Psychological Bulletin,* 1978, *85*, 1352-1375.

Johnston, J. M. Punishment of human behavior. *American Psychologist,* 1972, *27*, 1033-1054.

Review Set 6

1. P_____ is a procedure that decreases the future frequency of the behavior it follows.

2. Type I punishment is the a_____ of an aversive event following the misbehavior.

3. Type II punishment is the w_____ of a p_____ r_____ following the misbehavior.

4. The cardinal rule in using punishment is to always provide r_____ for an a_____ a_____ behavior.

5. You should always specify or define a c_____ by its e_____ on the behavior.

6. Punishment may i_____ suppress a behavior, may produce l_____ effects; may produce c_____ suppression; may teach o_____ not to perform a punished
   behavior; and may produce an i_____ effect.

7. The negative side effects of punishment are e_____
   behavior, a_____ towards the source of the punishment or others, n_____ modeling, and attempting to
   e_____ or a_____ the punishing person or situation.

8. A c_____ a_____ stimulus is a neutral stimulus
   that has acquired aversive properties because it has been
   repeatedly paired with a punishing event.

9. Punishment should be applied to a response in a behavior
   chain that is as far away from the t_____ reinforcer as
   possible.

The answers are on page 170.

CHAPTER 7

Timeout

From punishment in general we'll now turn to a specific punishment procedure, timeout. This is a procedure that's widely used with students. We'll begin by defining timeout and describing the two basic types, exclusionary and nonexclusionary, then cover the eight characteristics of a sound timeout program. Following this, the three types of exclusionary and three types of nonexclusionary timeout will be explained, as well as their advantages and disadvantages. We'll end by ranking exclusionary and nonexclusionary timeout in the Least Restrictive Treatment Model.

> Timeout is a Type II punishment procedure in which positive reinforcement is withdrawn for a prespecified period of time following the performance of a misbehavior.

There are two basic types of timeout: exclusionary and nonexclusionary. An exclusionary timeout procedure consists of removing the misbehaving student from the reinforcing environment for a specified period of time. The student may be placed in a timeout room or required either to remain behind a partition located in a corner of the classroom or living unit or to stand in the hallway. A nonexclusionary timeout procedure consists of allowing the student to remain in the reinforcing environment but not allowing her to engage in reinforcing activities for a specified period of time. Nonexclusionary timeout is accomplished by removing or withdrawing a specific reinforcer, by requiring the student to sit in a chair in the corner and observe her classmates receiving reinforcers, or by a timeout ribbon procedure (described shortly). Basically, the difference between these two types of timeout is that exclusionary timeout requires that the student be removed from the reinforcers while nonexclusionary timeout requires that the reinforcers be removed from the student.

CHARACTERISTICS OF A SOUND TIMEOUT PROGRAM

Before we discuss timeout procedures in detail, we must first talk about the common characteristics of any sound timeout program. The first and perhaps most important characteristic is that there must be a high density of reinforcement in the time-in area, that is, the classroom or living environment. This high density of reinforcement ensures that the timeout will be aversive and thereby effective because the student will be missing reinforcement opportunities while she is in timeout. The most common reason that timeout programs fail is that the density of reinforcement in the "reinforcing environment" is too low. As a result, there's not enough contrast between the reinforcing environment and timeout; the student is essentially in timeout in both conditions. This situation is most common in custodial institutions. The establishment of a high density of reinforcement in the classroom or during behavioral programming also minimizes the possibility that the student may misbehave in order to escape or avoid a stressful learning situation. Some students will actually misbehave in order to receive timeout, since they prefer the timeout over the required educational activity. This usually occurs when there are high response requirements associated with the activity, as when the student must actively respond, and little reinforcement available for performing the activity (a low density of reinforcement). However, if the density of reinforcement during the activity is high, the student will be less motivated to misbehave in order to escape or avoid it.

A second characteristic of a sound timeout program is that there's little, if any, reinforcement available to the student during the period she is in timeout. This, of course, maximizes the aversiveness of the timeout period, which is most humane since it will be effective in reducing the misbehavior quickly with the fewest possible applications needed.

A third characteristic is that the duration of the timeout is prespecified and relatively brief. Under normal circumstances the maximum period for any single timeout should be about 30 minutes. The general rule of thumb is the younger the student, the shorter the duration of timeout. Also, students who have lived in residential facilities typically require longer durations of timeout than those who live at home. At the end of the timeout, the student should be returned to the reinforcing environment, provided she is not misbehaving when the timeout interval ends. (We'll shortly discuss what to do in such cases.) Failure to specify the duration and keep it brief can result in abuses and misuses of timeout. For example, you may have read newspaper articles about so-called behavior modification programs in centers for juvenile delinquents. The articles probably noted the use of solitary confinement for several weeks and called that confinement "timeout." Clearly, that procedure was not timeout; it was an abuse of authority.

A fourth characteristic is that the student is not released from timeout if she is misbehaving when the timeout period ends. Releasing a misbehaving student from timeout is a major error because it pairs the student's misbehavior with release from timeout and such release could be reinforcing for the misbehaving student. The student could then be expected to misbehave each time she was timed out. To avoid this problem, the student is released from timeout at the end of the timeout period only if she isn't misbehaving. Thus, we're pairing release from timeout with appropriate behavior. If the student is misbehaving when the timeout period ends, recycle the timeout for a 1-minute interval and require that the student behave appropriately during the last 15 seconds of that interval. In other words, the student must not misbehave during the final 15 seconds of timeout in order to leave it. If she misbehaves, again continue for another minute and require appropriate behavior for the last 15 seconds. Under no circumstances should you recycle the entire timeout period if the student is misbehaving at the end of the timeout period except under exceptional circumstances. Otherwise the student might never get out.

A fifth characteristic is that the timeout is applied immediately following the misbehavior, as is the case for any punishment procedure.

Sixth, verbal interactions with the student are brief, to the point, stated in a neutral tone of voice, and paired with the word *no* (a conditioned aversive stimulus as discussed in Chapter 6). When the student misbehaves, simply say "No, you (name the misbehavior), and you must go into timeout." There's nothing else you need to say, except possibly "You can't leave timeout if you are (name the specific misbehavior[s])" and "You must stay here (specify the duration of timeout)." Limited verbal interactions while you institute the timeout will reduce the possibility that your attention will reinforce the student for misbehaving. While the student is in timeout, do *not* talk to her.

Seventh, efforts are taken to prevent "bootleg" reinforcement, which occurs when a student's classmates give her attention (social reinforcement) while she is in nonexclusionary timeout. Although this is more of a problem with moderately retarded and normal students, it can occur with severely and profoundly retarded students. If it does, the timeout program will lose much of its effectiveness because of the reinforcement the student is receiving while she is in timeout. To overcome such a problem, it may be necessary to implement negative consequences for those individuals providing the bootleg reinforcement or to use an exclusionary timeout procedure.

The eighth and final characteristic is that detailed records are kept. These records list the name of the student receiving timeout, the misbehavior that resulted in timeout, the time the student began timeout, the time the student was released from timeout, and the name of the staff person who instituted and terminated the timeout. (These records are especially important when a timeout room is being used.) Maintaining detailed timeout records will, in part, allow you to determine the effectiveness of the procedure and whether or not it's being used in an arbitrary and punitive fashion. Furthermore, these records will offer you some legal protection if something by chance goes awry.

Exclusionary timeout is generally considered to be more aversive than nonexclusionary timeout in the Least Restrictive Treatment Model. Written permission should be obtained from parents and administrators before using nonexclusionary procedures; in addition, permission should be obtained from the human rights or restrictive procedures committee before using exclusionary timeout procedures. Next we'll discuss exclusionary timeout so that the added advantages of nonexclusionary timeout can be compared to some of the disadvantages of exclusionary timeout.

Practice Set 7A

Answer the following questions.

1. What is the basic difference between exclusionary and nonexclusionary timeout?

2. What should be done if a student is misbehaving at the end of a timeout interval?

3. According to the Least Restrictive Treatment Model, which type of timeout is considered to be more aversive, exclusionary timeout or nonexclusionary timeout?

4. To ensure that a timeout program will be aversive and thereby effective, a h_____ d_____ of reinforcement must be provided.

5. If possible, there should be no r_____ available to the student when she is in timeout.

6. To use timeout properly, the d_____ of timeout should be prespecified and it should be relatively b_____.

7. A student should never be released from timeout if she is m_____.

8. To be effective, timeout should be applied i_____ following the misbehavior.

9. In a timeout program, all verbal interactions with the student should be brief, to the point, stated in a n_____ tone of voice, and paired with the word _____.

10. B_____ reinforcement occurs when a misbehaving student's classmates give her attention while she is in timeout.

11. In any sound timeout program, detailed r_____ must be kept.

12. W_____ p_____ must be obtained from parents and administrators before using nonexclusionary timeout and in addition from human rights or restrictive procedures committees before using exclusionary timeout.

Answers are found on page 170.

EXCLUSIONARY TIMEOUT

There are three ways to use exclusionary timeout: (1) remove the student to a timeout room, (2) place the student behind a partition that is located in a corner of the classroom or living area, or (3) require the student to stand in the hallway outside the reinforcing environment.

Timeout in a Timeout Room

A timeout room is a relatively small room devoid of any reinforcing stimuli; the room is bare. The ideal timeout room is located adjacent to the classroom or nearby, has good lighting and ventilation, and a window (made of plexiglass) or one-way-vision mirror on the door to permit unobtrusive observations of the student. In some cases it's highly advisable to pad the floor and walls of the room. This can be accomplished with gym mats or carpeting that has several thicknesses of padding under it. A record sheet (described earlier) should hang on the outside of the timeout room door or on a nearby wall. The following example illustrates the use of a timeout room.

Robby, the self-abuser, occasionally hit other children. To reduce this behavior, Ms. Hodos decided to use a timeout room. The next time Robby hit a classmate, Ms. Hodos said, in a neutral tone of voice, "No, you hit Charlie, you must go to the timeout room." Ms. Hodos quickly took Robby's hand and rapidly escorted him to a nearby timeout room. She opened the door, placed Robby in the room, said, "You must stay here 10 minutes," and closed the door. She then recorded the time, Robby's name, her name, and the misbehavior on the record sheet that was hanging on the door. Ten minutes later, Ms. Hodos observed that Robby was not misbehaving, opened the door, and said, "You can come out now and go back to class." She recorded the time she let Robby out of timeout on the record sheet and then escorted him back to class. Within 2 weeks, the contingent use of the timeout room had eliminated Robby's hitting others.

The advantages associated with using a timeout room are:

1. The disruptive student is removed from the reinforcing environment, thereby increasing the possibility that the timeout will be aversive.
2. The timeout room is devoid of any reinforcing stimuli, so there are few, if any, reinforcers available to the student while he is in timeout.
3. There's no possibility of bootleg reinforcement.
4. Entrance in and exit out of the room provide the student with a clear signal as to when timeout is in effect.
5. Highly agitated students can be removed from the classroom, thereby eliminating the possibility that they might injure someone, destroy property, or disrupt the educational activities of the other students.

The disadvantages of a timeout room procedure are:

1. It's difficult, if not impossible, to institute the timeout immediately since the student must be taken to the timeout room.
2. A special room must be set up to function as the timeout room, which can present difficulties when room space is at a premium.
3. There's the distinct possibility that the student may receive some attention for his misbehavior during the process of taking him to the timeout room. For example, if the student

becomes combative while you are attempting to take him to the timeout room, you'll be providing him with attention in your efforts to overcome his resistance. He could also be receiving attention from his classmates while you are grappling with him.

4. The continuity of the classroom educational tasks is interrupted. Whenever a student is to be placed in a timeout room, one of the staff must escort him there. That person must immediately terminate whatever she is doing with her students so that she can institute the timeout program. Thus, when the timeout room is used frequently, the daily classroom schedule can be disrupted by the frequent absences of the staff.

5. The procedure can only be used in those situations in which a timeout room is available. As a result, it's difficult to program for generalization of the procedure. For instance, what would you do on a field trip when the student misbehaves?

6. The procedure is less likely to be effective for those students who enjoy being alone (self-isolates), who engage in high rates of self-stimulatory behavior, or who masturbate frequently. To overcome this problem, you must ensure that the classroom contains a high density of reinforcement.

7. While in timeout, the student may engage in behaviors that require you to enter the timeout room and intervene. For example, if the student becomes self-abusive, rips his clothing off, or smears feces on the walls, you must intervene to interrupt these behaviors. (This would be especially true in the case of self-abuse, where the student's well-being is threatened.) By doing so, you're providing the student with attention (social reinforcement) and hence may nullify the effectiveness of the timeout program. It's entirely possible that the student may display such bizarre behaviors because he has little else to do in the timeout room. Thus, the student has more control in the timeout room than it might first appear. It's fortunate for us that only a relatively small number of students engage in such bizarre behaviors while they are in timeout. Nevertheless, it's a potential problem that you may encounter.

8. There is the remote possibility that the timeout room could be used for staff convenience. This occurs when a staff member uses the room simply to "get the student out of the way for a while" rather than for a prespecified misbehavior. Such staff behavior is not only arbitrary but punitive and must not be tolerated.

Timeout Behind a Partition in the Classroom

A timeout area can be created by partitioning off a corner of the classroom. Ideally, the partitions should be stable enough and placed so that the student cannot move them or knock them over. Often the record sheet can be hung on the partition.

The timeout area procedure essentially offers the same advantages as the timeout room with one notable exception. The student may receive bootleg reinforcement because she may be able to generate sufficient noise to disturb her classmates and thereby gain their attention. In fact, if she's loud enough, she may be able to disturb the classroom routine. The timeout area does, however, offer one major advantage over the timeout room: it allows the procedure to be implemented more quickly. Also, it doesn't require the use of a special room or disrupt the continuity of the educational activities as much as a timeout room procedure does. The timeout area does suffer from the other disadvantages listed for the timeout room.

Timeout in the Hallway

This is a seldom-used form of exclusionary timeout and there's a very good reason why. In addition to having the disadvantages already listed, the misbehaving student can run away or go into other classrooms or living units and cause a disturbance. As a result, a student should not be timed out in the hallway unless (1) she's quite docile and under good instructional control, meaning she'll follow your instructions to remain in the hallway, and (2) the duration of timeout is quite brief, usually 5 minutes or less.

Practice Set 7B

Answer the following questions.

1. Name three ways of using exclusionary timeout.
2. List five advantages associated with using a timeout room.
3. List eight disadvantages associated with using a timeout room.
4. List one disadvantage of timeout behind a partition that it doesn't share with a timeout room. List three advantages that the procedure does not share with a timeout room procedure.
5. List the two criteria for using a hallway timeout procedure. What's the major disadvantage of this procedure?

Answers are found on pages 170 and 171.

NONEXCLUSIONARY TIMEOUT

There are three ways to use nonexclusionary timeout: (1) withdrawing a specific reinforcer, (2) requiring the student to sit in a corner of the classroom, or (3) using the timeout ribbon procedure.

Timeout by Withdrawing a Specific Reinforcer

This type of nonexclusionary timeout is useful when the student misbehaves during a specific activity in which a very powerful reinforcer is available to her. For example, if a student attempts to eat with her fingers during mealtime, you can time her out simply by removing her plate of food for a minute or two. Because the food is a powerful reinforcer and an integral part of the educational activity of teaching appropriate table manners, the inappropriate eating behavior should be suppressed quickly. Another example would be a student who is misbehaving while playing with her favorite toy. Removing the toy for a brief period contingent on the misbehavior should produce a rapid decrease in that misbehavior.

The advantages of this timeout procedure are:

1. Timeout can be implemented immediately.
2. The student sees what she is missing, which should help to make the procedure aversive (punishing).
3. The presence or absence of the reinforcer provides a clear signal as to when timeout is in effect.
4. No special room or area is required.
5. There's little chance that bootleg reinforcement will be a problem, since the reinforcer from which the student is being timed out should be more powerful for the student than attention from her classmates. Also, there's less chance that your attention will reinforce any misbehavior because you're not required to escort the student anywhere.
6. There's less interruption of the classroom routine, since the timeout is implemented in the learning environment.
7. The procedure can be used in a variety of locations and situations. For instance, timing a student out from her plate of food can be accomplished in any situation in which the food is available.
8. There's less chance that the student will misbehave during the timeout period. The student quickly learns that if she misbehaves during timeout, she'll only be delaying her access to the powerful reinforcer.

9. The procedure may be effective with self-isolates, self-stimulators, and masturbators because those reinforcing behaviors are competing with a powerful reinforcer (the timed-out reinforcer) for which the student may be highly deprived.

10. There's less chance that the procedure will be used in an arbitrary or punitive fashion.

The disadvantages of the procedure are:

1. The student may become agitated and/or combative when the reinforcer is removed. If her agitation is serious enough, some type of backup such as a timeout room may be required.

2. The student may disturb her classmates because she is remaining in the educational environment.

3. The success of the procedure is dependent on having a powerful reinforcer for the student and a sufficient level of deprivation related to that reinforcer.

Timeout by Requiring the Student to Sit in a Corner

This is a general type of nonexclusionary timeout that can be used for a variety of misbehaviors. The procedure can be implemented in either of two ways. One way is to require the student to sit in a chair located in a corner of the room during her timeout. This is sometimes called a timeout chair procedure. The other way (sometimes called contingent observation) is simply to require the student to sit or remain on the perimeter of the room during timeout. The only real difference between the two is that the timeout chair procedure specifies where the student must be during the timeout period. The rationale underlying both procedures is that the student may be learning appropriate forms of behavior by observing her classmates during her timeout.

Ms. Hodos has decided to try a timeout chair procedure to punish Robby when he hits his classmates. Whenever Robby hits someone, Ms. Hodos says, "No, you hit Charlie, you must go sit in the timeout chair." She then quickly takes Robby's hand and rapidly escorts him to a chair located in a corner of the classroom. She seats Robby and tells him, "You must sit here for 5 minutes." Ms. Hodos returns to her desk, fills out her timeout record sheet, and then begins working with the other students and reinforcing their appropriate responses. Five minutes later, she returns to Robby and tells him he may return to his desk.

These two procedures—the timeout chair procedure and contingent observation—offer the same advantages and disadvantages as timeout by withdrawing a specific reinforcer, with the following exceptions. Additional advantages of these procedures are:

1. They can be used to punish a variety of misbehaviors.
2. Positive modeling may take place. If the timed-out student observes her classmates behaving appropriately and receiving reinforcers for such behaviors, she may imitate those positive behaviors when she is returned to the reinforcing environment.
3. The student won't miss the ongoing educational activities because she can still observe them.

The additional disadvantages are:

1. The student may not stay seated in the chair or on the perimeter of the room.
2. Because no single powerful reinforcer is involved, there's a greater chance that bootleg reinforcement may nullify the procedure, or that self-isolates, self-stimulators, or masturbators will find the timeout period to be reinforcing.

Timeout by Using the Timeout Ribbon Procedure

The timeout ribbon procedure offers some distinct advantages over the other nonexclusionary timeout procedures, as we'll see shortly. It can be used with one student, a few students, or an entire class. When it is used with all of your students, the program is set up as follows.

All the students in the classroom are given a ribbon to wear on their wrists. Each ribbon is a different color so that the ribbons are individualized. Whenever a student is reinforced, the instructor describes the appropriate behavior and mentions the fact that the student is wearing his ribbon—"Good, Dave, you're looking at me and wearing your ribbon." Pairing the requirement that the ribbon be worn with the delivery of reinforcers establishes the ribbon (a neutral stimulus) as a discriminative stimulus for reinforcement and hence a conditioned reinforcer. Over time the students learn that they must be wearing their ribbons in order to receive any reinforcement.

Once the ribbons have been established as a prerequisite for reinforcement (you'll know that the ribbons have acquired reinforcing properties when the students cease trying to remove them), the timeout procedure is implemented. Whenever a student misbehaves, the instructor removes the student's ribbon and says, for example, "No, Dave, you're screaming, you can't have your ribbon." The ribbon is removed for a specified period (the timeout interval) and all forms of instructor-dispensed reinforcement and student participation in classroom activities are discontinued. At the end of the timeout period, the ribbon is returned, provided that the student isn't misbehaving.

The timeout ribbon procedure offers all of the advantages of the other two nonexclusionary timeout procedures as well as these additional benefits:

1. Group treatment is possible. The timeout procedure can be implemented at any time with any and all students who have misbehaved. Thus, there's no problem of running out of timeout rooms, partitions, chairs, or corners.

2. Bootleg reinforcement can be quickly terminated because all you need to do is remove the ribbon(s) of the student(s) who is providing attention to his misbehaving classmate.

3. Any bizarre misbehaviors that the student performs during his timeout such as self-abuse can be interrupted early in the response chain. You can simply stop the misbehavior without commenting or looking at the student. There is less danger that you'll be reinforcing the misbehavior because you're already in the timeout situation with the student.

4. The presence or absence of the ribbon provides a clear signal to visitors as to when it's appropriate to interact with a student. One of the major problems that can occur during the use of a reductive procedure such as extinction or nonexclusionary timeout is that a visitor may inadvertently reinforce the student on extinction or in timeout with attention. The timeout ribbon procedure, however, eliminates this problem, since visitors can learn not to attend to anyone who isn't wearing a ribbon. To aid visitors in learning this discrimination, place a large sign outside the classroom or unit door that explains the purpose of the timeout ribbon procedure. By doing so, you won't have to intercept each visitor to explain who is allowed social interaction and who isn't.

5. The highly visible ribbons serve as a reminder to staff members to reinforce their students. Similarly, the absence of the ribbon helps staff members to remember who's in timeout and when they should be released.

6. The procedure can be used across settings (across classes, at home and school, at school and in a residential setting)

because the student can *always* wear the ribbon. This benefit makes it an excellent procedure to teach to parents, which helps ensure a consistent programming effort throughout the student's waking hours.

7. There's no concern about keeping the timed-out student in one location, as is the case with some of the other nonexclusionary timeout procedures.

Aside from sharing the disadvantages already noted for nonexclusionary timeout procedures, the timeout ribbon has one additional disadvantage. Because the timed-out student is free to move about the room, he can possibly destroy property; for example, he could rip pictures off the wall. One way to minimize this problem is to keep all teaching materials in locked cabinets unless they are being used in the current activity and to ensure that objects on the walls are either firmly attached, indestructible, or expendable. Of course, this behavior can be stopped as described in 3 by interrupting the maladaptive response chain.

The key to the success of a timeout ribbon procedure is that the ribbon be established as a requirement for reinforcement. Other objects can also be used in the same fashion as the ribbon, such as a happy face button or some type of tag. However, ribbon wrist bands with Velcro tape on each end are preferable to tags or buttons because wrist bands are less obtrusive and therefore fit in better with the spirit of normalization. To ensure that the object chosen acquires reinforcing properties, you must provide liberal amounts of reinforcement when you are beginning the program. Along this line, the frequency of reinforcement must be shorter than the timeout interval. If the timeout period is 3 minutes, reinforcement should be delivered to the other students about every 2 minutes. By doing this, you will be ensuring that the timed-out student misses at least one reinforcement opportunity and thus is really in timeout!

Practice Set 7C

Answer the following questions.

1. List three ways of using nonexclusionary timeout.
2. List the ten advantages of timing a student out by withdrawing a specific reinforcer.
3. List the three disadvantages of timing a student out by withdrawing a specific reinforcer.
4. List three advantages of timing a student out in a corner that it doesn't share with the timeout procedure of withdrawing a specific reinforcer.

5. List two disadvantages of timing a student out in a corner that it doesn't share with the timeout procedure of withdrawing a specific reinforcer.

6. List seven advantages of the timeout ribbon procedure that it doesn't share with the other nonexclusionary timeout methods.

7. List the one disadvantage of the timeout ribbon procedure that it doesn't share with the other nonexclusionary timeout methods.

The answers are on pages 171-173.

THE LEAST RESTRICTIVE TREATMENT MODEL

We've now discussed nine procedures that will decrease an undesirable behavior and have grouped them into three levels within the Least Restrictive Treatment Model. Level 1 procedures contain no aversive or intrusive properties, while Level 2 procedures do contain some aversive or intrusive properties. Although Level 2 procedures are not very restrictive of the student's rights, you still should obtain written approval from your administration and the student or his parents or guardian before using a Level 2 procedure. Level 3 procedures are quite aversive and intrusive. Their use requires written permission from the student or his parents, the administration, and the human rights committee.

Level 1	Level 2	Level 3
DRO (Differential Reinforcement of Other Behavior)	Negative practice (when manual guidance is not given)	Negative practice (when manual guidance is given)
DRA (Differential Reinforcement of Appropriate Behavior)	Extinction	Physical restraint
DRI (Differential Reinforcement of Incompatible Behavior)	Nonexclusionary timeout	Exclusionary timeout
Satiation		

SUMMARY

Timeout is a Type II punishment procedure in which positive reinforcement is withdrawn for a prespecified period of time following the performance of the misbehavior. There are two types of timeout, exclusionary and nonexclusionary. In exclusionary timeout, the student is removed from the reinforcers; in nonexclusionary timeout, the reinforcers are removed from the student.

There are eight common characteristics of any sound timeout program. (1) There must be a high density of reinforcement in the classroom or living environment. (2) Little, if any, reinforcement must be available during timeout. (3) The duration of timeout must be prespecified and brief. (4) The student must not be released if she is misbehaving when timeout ends. (5) Timeout must be applied immediately. (6) Verbal interactions must be kept brief and to the point, be stated in a neutral tone of voice, and be paired with the word *no*. (7) Bootleg reinforcement must be prevented. (8) Detailed records of the use of timeout must be kept.

There are three ways to use exclusionary timeout: (1) remove the student to a timeout room, (2) place the student behind a partition located in a corner of the room, and (3) require the student to stand in the hallway. There are also three ways to use nonexclusionary timeout: (1) withdraw a specific reinforcer such as food, (2) require the student to sit in a corner or on the periphery of the room, and (3) use the timeout ribbon procedure (the removal of a stimulus that has been associated with reinforcement).

Exclusionary timeout procedures are highly aversive and are therefore considered to be Level 3 procedures in the Least Restrictive Treatment Model, whereas nonexclusionary procedures are less aversive and are therefore considered to be Level 2 procedures.

SUGGESTED READINGS

Bostow, D. E., & Bailey, J. B. Modification of severe disruptive and aggressive behavior using brief timeout and reinforcement procedures. *Journal of Applied Behavior Analysis*, 1969, *2*, 31-37.

Foxx, R. M., & Shapiro, S. T. The timeout ribbon: A nonexclusionary timeout procedure. *Journal of Applied Behavior Analysis*, 1978, *11*, 125-136.

Hamilton, J., Stephens, L., & Allen, P. Controlling aggressive and destructive behavior in severely retarded institutionalized residents. *American Journal of Mental Deficiency*, 1967, *71*, 852-856.

Pendergrass, V. E. Timeout from positive reinforcement following persistent, high-rate behavior in retardates. *Journal of Applied Behavior Analysis*, 1972, *5*, 85-92.

Porterfield, J. K., Herbert-Jackson, E., & Risley, T. R. Contingent observation: An effective and acceptable procedure for reducing disruptive behavior of young children in a group setting. *Journal of Applied Behavior Analysis*, 1976, 5, 85-92.

White, G. D., Nielsen, G., & Johnson, G. M. Timeout duration and the suppression of deviant behavior in children. *Journal of Applied Behavior Analysis*, 1972, 5, 111-120.

Review Set 7

1. T_____ is a Type II punishment procedure in which positive reinforcement is withdrawn for a prespecified period of time following the performance of the misbehavior.

2. An e_____ timeout procedure consists of removing the misbehaving student from the reinforcing environment.

3. A n_____ timeout procedure consists of allowing the misbehaving student to remain in the reinforcing environment but not allowing her to engage in reinforcing activities.

4. The entire timeout period should be recycled if the student is misbehaving at the end of the timeout period. True or False

5. The three ways of using exclusionary timeout are to (a) remove the student to a t_____ room, (b) place the student behind a p_____ located in a corner of the classroom, and (c) require the student to stand in the h_____.

6. The ideal timeout room is located near the classroom, has good lighting and ventilation, and a window made of plexiglass or a one-way-vision mirror to permit unobtrusive observation of the student. True or False

7. The three ways of using nonexclusionary timeout are (a) withdrawing a s_____ reinforcer, (b) requiring the student to sit in a corner of the room, and (c) using the t_____ r_____ procedure.

8. In the timeout c_____ procedure, the student is required to sit in a chair located in the corner of the room.

9. In c_____ o_____, the student is required to sit on the perimeter of the room during her timeout.

10. When beginning a timeout ribbon program, the frequency of reinforcement must be s_____ than the timeout interval.

11. Because they are highly aversive and intrusive, e_____ timeout procedures are Level _____ procedures in the

Least Restrictive Treatment Model, whereas nonexclusionary timeout procedures are Level _____ procedures.

Answers are found on page 173.

CHAPTER 8

Overcorrection

We continue covering punishment procedures by discussing overcorrection, a Type I punishment procedure widely used with retarded and autistic students. If you're familiar at all with overcorrection, you're aware that many labels have been given to the various overcorrection procedures. This use of multiple labels has caused some confusion. Accordingly, we've dispensed with the use of labels in this chapter and instead simply defined the various techniques that have been generated by the overcorrection rationale.

To begin this chapter, overcorrection will be defined and its two components will be explained. We'll then talk about the three characteristics of overcorrection acts and the four common elements of all overcorrection programs. After citing examples of overcorrection acts and programs, and showing how overcorrection promotes the normalization of retarded students, we'll list the advantages and disadvantages of overcorrection. Finally, the overcorrection procedure will be ranked in the Least Restrictive Treatment Model.

> Overcorrection is a Type I punishment procedure in which the misbehaving student is required to overcorrect the environmental effects of her misbehavior and/or to practice appropriate forms of behavior in those situations in which the misbehavior commonly occurs.

The general rationale of overcorrection is to require the misbehaving student (1) to overcorrect the environmental effects of the inappropriate act, and (2) to practice overly correct forms of relevant behavior in those situations where the misbehavior commonly occurs. The first objective is accomplished by having the student restore the disturbed situation to a state vastly improved from that existing prior to the disruption. To determine what the student should be required to do for this component, first *identify the specific and general disturbances that resulted from the misbehavior and then identify the behaviors needed to vastly improve the results of the misbehavior.* Once you've determined those corrective actions, you then require the misbehaving student to perform them whenever she misbehaves. For example, a student who overturned a desk would first be required to return the desk to its correct position and then to dust and wax it. After that, she would be required to straighten and dust all other desks in the room.

The second objective is accomplished by having the student repeatedly practice appropriate behaviors in the situation in which she normally misbehaves. This component can possibly serve an educative function because it may teach the student alternative appropriate ways of responding. (Note: No reinforcement is delivered during the overcorrection; otherwise, the student might misbehave in order to receive the overcorrection punishment procedure.) To determine what the misbehaving student should be required to do in a particular overcorrection consequence, you must *identify appropriate behaviors that should be practiced* and then require the student to perform them whenever she misbehaves. For this component, the overcorrection procedure for overturning a desk would be to perform an appropriate behavior while seated at the desk, such as coloring or working a puzzle. Thus, the purpose of the overcorrection would be to teach the student some of the appropriate behaviors associated with a desk.

The two overcorrection components can be combined and applied as one procedure or applied singly. The misbehaviors for which only one of the components is used will be discussed shortly. At this point, let's look at an example of overcorrection in use.

Ms. Hodos has decided to design an overcorrection procedure to treat Robby's self-abusive behavior. She first identifies the specific and general disturbances that result from the self-abuse. As you may recall, Robby self-abuses by striking the sides of his head with his fists. The specific disturbance or consequence of his self-abuse is that the sides of his head are covered with large, swollen red welts. The general environmental disturbance is that Robby becomes agitated when he hits himself and this agitation prevents him from attending to educational activities and disturbs his classmates and his instructors. Ms. Hodos identifies the behaviors to be required of Robby in order to vastly improve the situation. She decides to treat the specific problem of the swelling caused by the blows by using an ice pack. Whenever

Robby hits himself, she'll require him to hold an ice pack on his head where the blow was delivered. The use of the ice pack will accomplish two purposes: (1) it will reduce the swelling caused by the blow, and (2) it will serve as an aversive or negative consequence for self-abuse since feeling cold is aversive to most people. To treat the general problem of Robby's agitation, Ms. Hodos decides that whenever Robby hits himself, she'll require him to lie quietly on a mat until he becomes calm. While lying on the mat, he'll also be required to hold the ice pack to his head. Requiring Robby to lie on the mat will accomplish two purposes: (1) it will reduce his agitation and might teach him how to relax, and (2) it will serve as an aversive consequence since it constitutes a timeout from reinforcement. (How such a procedure could serve as a timeout period will be discussed shortly.)

Having designed the first component, Ms. Hodos is ready to design the second by identifying the alternative appropriate behaviors that Robby will be required to repeatedly practice. Because Robby hits himself with his fists, it's apparent to Ms. Hodos that he must be required to use his hands for appropriate activities. She decides that she wants to bring Robby's use of his hands under external control (her control). In other words, she wants Robby to use his hands under direction rather than to hit himself as he usually chooses to do. To gain this external control, Ms. Hodos decides that she'll require him to move his arms into one of three positions when she instructs him to do so. Specifically, she'll require Robby to lift his arms above his head, out from his sides, and directly in front of him. Robby would be required to sustain each position for 15 seconds and the entire sequence of positions would be repeated until 10 minutes had elapsed.

Ms. Hodos has designed the overcorrection program to treat Robby's self-abuse. However, before she begins using the program, she must first take a baseline (see Chapter 9) and also ensure that there is a high density of reinforcement available to Robby when he behaves appropriately, as when he is working at an educational task. Because of the nature and severity of Robby's misbehavior, Ms. Hodos conducted a brief 1-day baseline that consisted of time sampling Robby's hitting every 5 minutes (see Chapter 9). Robby had been wearing a football helmet up until the time Ms. Hodos began the baseline. During the baseline, she removed Robby's helmet for 1 minute every 5 minutes. Following this 1-minute observation interval, she replaced the helmet until she was ready for the next observation interval 4 minutes later. Her baseline revealed that, without the helmet, Robby hit himself 92% of the time.

The first day of overcorrection Ms. Hodos removed Robby's helmet and prepared to punish his self-abuse with the overcorrection program. The first time Robby hit himself, she said, "No, Robby, don't hit yourself" and restrained his hands with hers. She quickly guided him to a mat located beside his desk and then guided him in lying flat on his back (she held his hands throughout in order to prevent him from hitting himself). While Ms. Hodos held Robby on the mat, her aide, Ms. Levine, brought over an ice pack from the refrigerator. Ms. Levine placed the ice pack in Robby's right hand, which Ms. Hodos then guided to his head. Ms. Hodos held Robby's hand so that he couldn't drop the ice pack. Meanwhile, Ms. Levine held Robby's ankles because he'd begun kicking in an attempt to get up from the mat. Both Ms. Hodos and Ms. Levine avoided looking directly at Robby's eyes so that they wouldn't be giving him any eye contact and hence any attention. Neither spoke. Whenever Robby ceased resisting and became relaxed, they relaxed their grips on his hands and ankles. When he resumed struggling, they both once again held him firmly. After 5 minutes, they let Robby up. (They did not let him up, however, until he appeared to be relaxed.) Holding Robby's hands, Ms. Hodos escorted him back to his chair and guided him in sitting down. She then began requiring him to move his arms.

Standing behind Robby, Ms. Hodos instructed him to raise his arms above his head by stating in a neutral tone of voice, "Hands up." Because Robby did not react to the instruction within a few seconds, she guided his arms above his head and required him to hold that position for 15 seconds. At the end of the 15 seconds, she said, "Hands in front," and since he did not respond, she gently guided his arms out in front of him. He was required to hold this position for 15 seconds, after which she said, "Hands down." Again, she had to guide Robby's arms into the position since he wouldn't respond to the instruction.

Ms. Hodos continued to require Robby to move his arms into one of the three positions every 15 seconds. She presented the instructions randomly so that he'd have to attend to each specific instruction, rather than simply learn a sequence of movements. Whenever he struggled, she prevented him from moving his arms. Whenever he relaxed his arms, she relaxed her hands but kept them in contact with his arms. She never instructed him to move his arms to another position if he was struggling at the end of the 15-second interval. Rather, she waited until he had ceased struggling before she gave the instruction. (She didn't want to pair his struggling with being allowed to move; rather, she wanted Robby to learn that he could only move when he was instructed to do so and not struggling.) Ms. Hodos had Robby move through the various arm positions until 10 minutes had elapsed.

The complete overcorrection program lasted 15 minutes: 5 minutes of lying on the mat with the ice pack and 10 minutes of arm guidance. At the end of the 15 minutes, Ms. Hodos released Robby's arms and said, "Now, don't hit yourself." She then guided his hands to a task that required fine motor movements, released them, waited 10 seconds, and then reinforced him with a piece of a potato stick.

Ms. Hodos used the complete overcorrection program immediately following each instance of self-abuse. After 2 weeks, Robby's self-abusive behavior had been reduced to a near zero level. At that point, Ms. Hodos reduced the duration of the overcorrection to 5 minutes (2 minutes of lying on the mat with the ice pack and 3 minutes of arm movements). When Robby's self-abuse was ultimately reduced to zero during the next week, she instituted a verbal warning procedure. In that procedure each day, Robby was warned the first time he hit himself, "Robby, don't hit yourself." If he didn't hit himself again, no overcorrection was given. However, if he did hit himself a second time, he received a 5-minute overcorrection procedure. Eventually Robby ceased hitting himself in the classroom.

Ms. Hodos noticed several changes in Robby's behavior over the course of the overcorrection program. The first was that he ultimately learned to move his arms in the instructed direction. The second was that he stopped struggling while he was on the mat or when he was required to move his arms. The third was that he became more attentive in the classroom to both her and Ms. Levine and to some of the classroom stimulus materials. Because of these changes and the elimination of Robby's self-abuse, Ms. Hodos felt that the amount of time she had invested in the overcorrection program had been worthwhile.

Now let's find out why Ms. Hodos' overcorrection program was successful. The following sections discuss the nature of overcorrection and how it can be effectively used.

Practice Set 8A

Answer the following questions.

1. O_____ is a procedure in which the misbehaving student is required to overcorrect the environmental effects of his misbehavior and/or to practice appropriate forms of behavior in those situations in which the misbehavior commonly occurs.

2. In one overcorrection component, the student is required to

restore the disturbed environment to a vastly improved state. True or False

3. In the other overcorrection component the student is required to repeatedly practice inappropriate behaviors in the situation in which he normally misbehaves. True or False

4. The two overcorrection components must be used together. True or False

Answers are found on page 173.

CHARACTERISTICS OF OVERCORRECTION ACTS

Any overcorrection acts the student must perform are designed to have the following characteristics.

They're directly related to the student's misbehavior. As a result there's less chance that an instructor will use overcorrection in an arbitrary or punitive way. For instance, it's easy for an instructor to place a student in a timeout room if the student is "getting on his nerves." This same instructor, however, is much less likely to use overcorrection out of frustration because he must spend the overcorrection time ensuring that the student performs the required overcorrection acts. Furthermore, the fact that the overcorrection acts are related to the misbehavior means that the misbehaving student directly experiences the effort that her instructors have had to expend in the past in order to correct the results of her misbehavior. For example, a student who throws a cup of milk on the floor would be required as part of her overcorrection to mop up not only the spill, but also a portion of the floor. This wouldn't happen using any other inhibitory procedure, since the instructors would probably implement the consequence (perhaps take the student to the timeout room) and then clean up the spill themselves.

Like all effective punishment procedures, overcorrection is implemented immediately following the misbehavior. This immediate application leaves the student with little time to enjoy (be reinforced by) the results of her misbehavior and thus constitutes an extinction trial. To take one example, many theorists believe that one of the reinforcers for aggression towards another person is the aggressor seeing the pain and discomfort she has caused her victim. Thus, the victim's eyes welling with tears or her face contorting in pain might serve as reinforcers for the attacker's aggression. However, if the attacker were immediately required to comfort and administer to her victim through an overcorrection procedure, the reinforcing aspects associated with the aggressive act would be greatly diminished.

The overcorrection acts must be performed rapidly. This rapid performance also contributes to the aversiveness of overcorrection, because most people find it aversive to be required to work rapidly. Your use of physical guidance permits you to minimize the use of verbal instructions, since you use the physical guidance to ensure that the instructions are completed. This is accomplished by physically guiding the student's limbs through the requested movements, with only enough guidance used to ensure that the desired act is completed. The technical term for this manual guidance procedure is graduated guidance.

> Graduated guidance is a technique combining physical guidance and fading in which the physical guidance is systematically and gradually reduced and faded according to the student's responsiveness.

Graduated guidance is used to ensure that the misbehaving student performs the overcorrection acts. The major difference between graduated guidance and manual guidance (as in physical prompting) is that in graduated guidance the amount of the instructor's physical guidance (hand pressure) is adjusted from moment to moment depending on the student's performance (behavior) at that moment.

There are three parts to the graduated guidance technique: full graduated guidance, partial graduated guidance, and shadowing. These three parts reflect the amount of trainer participation in the student's performance of a particular sequence of behaviors. One part or all parts may be used during any overcorrection session. Graduated guidance is used as follows:*

1. Exert no more force at any given moment than is needed to move the student's hand in the desired direction.
2. At the start of each overcorrection, use the minimal force (even a touch) and build up until the hand starts moving.
3. Once the hand starts to move, decrease the guidance instantly and gradually as long as the guided hand continues to move.
4. If movement stops during a session, increase the guiding

---

*Adapted with permission from *Toilet training the retarded: A rapid program for day and nighttime independent toileting* by R. M. Foxx and N. H. Azrin. Champaign, Ill.: Research Press, 1973, pp. 37-38.

force instantly and gradually to the point where movement again results.

5. If the guided hand pushes against you in the direction away from the proper motion, apply just enough force to counteract that force, thereby keeping the resisting hand in a nonmoving position.

6. As soon as the resisting hand decreases the degree of opposing force, instantly decrease the amount of force so that the student's resistance is again just being counterbalanced.

7. When the guided hand stops actively resisting, immediately but gradually start again to use just enough force to move the guided hand.

8. Once a session starts, continue to guide the hand until the response is completed; do not give up or interrupt before the final step.

During *full graduated guidance*, the instructor keeps his hands in full contact with the student's hands. If the student should resist the full graduated guidance, the instructor would use just enough force to counteract the student's resistance and reduce and then eliminate this force when the student ceased resisting. As the student allows her hands to be guided without any resistance, the instructor begins using *partial graduated guidance*. During the partial graduated guidance, the instructor merely guides the student's hands with his thumb and forefinger. In this way the instructor fades the amount of physical contact so that the student takes more responsibility for the guided behaviors.

If the student does not resist the instructor's use of partial graduated guidance, the instructor begins using *shadowing*. During shadowing the instructor keeps his hands within an inch of the student's hands throughout the behavioral sequence. If the student stops at any time during the overcorrection session, the instructor reapplies partial or full graduated guidance (depending on which is necessary to motivate the student to perform the desired action) until the student once again begins the action; at that point the instructor resumes the shadowing. The use of shadowing permits the instructor to fade his physical contact so that it no longer serves as a physical prompt. In this way the student begins to attend only to the instructor's verbal instructions.

Within each overcorrection session you can use all three parts of the graduated guidance technique. Your choice of whether to use full graduated guidance, partial graduated guidance, or shadowing depends on what the student is doing at the moment. For example, you might begin using full graduated guidance, then switch to partial graduated guidance as the student begins taking over some of the desired action, and then begin shadowing when the student is performing the action. If the student should stop the action at any time, guidance would be reapplied (either full or partial, whichever was necessary) until the student resumed the action, at which time you would resume the shadowing. For any instances of resistance, you would use only the amount of hand force necessary to counterbalance the resistive action.

Over time you may be able to eliminate the full graduated guidance, then the partial guidance, until you only need to shadow the student's hands during the activity. On the other hand, some students may require full graduated guidance each time overcorrection is used, while others may require all three parts at various times throughout the overcorrection session.

COMMON ELEMENTS IN OVERCORRECTION PROGRAMS

Although a specific overcorrection program is designed for each specific misbehavior, there are several elements common to all overcorrection programs.

The use of a verbal reprimand. Immediately following the misbehavior, the student is told *no* and what he did wrong—"No, you hit Rita!" The word *no* is used because it's a conditioned aversive stimulus, a neutral stimulus that has been repeatedly paired with punishing stimuli until it has acquired negative or punishing properties. This use of the word *no* facilitates generalization across settings and may temporarily suppress or interrupt any ongoing behavior. The description of the misbehavior—"You hit Rita"—serves as negative feedback to the misbehaving student.

A period of timeout from positive reinforcement. The misbehaving student's ongoing activities are terminated and there's little if any time to engage in activities that may be reinforcing during the performance of the overcorrection acts.

Short verbal instructions delivered once in a neutral tone of voice. The instructions you give the student that inform him of the various corrective actions he is to perform and your mere presence during the overcorrection (you're with the student the entire time) could be sources of attention. As a result, there are several steps you must take in order to minimize this attention: (1)

give each instruction only once, and if the student doesn't respond within a few seconds, manually guide him in carrying out the instructed response, (2) make each instruction as brief as possible, and, (3) most importantly, deliver each instruction in a neutral tone of voice in order to minimize its reinforcement value. Many retarded students respond to a stern, loud tone of voice as if it were reinforcing, possibly because many of their previous interactions with people have consisted of people shouting or becoming angry with them. Because our voice inflection appears to play a major role in determining how reinforcing our voices are, giving instructions in a robot-like manner during overcorrection (no inflection or affect) will minimize their social reinforcement value.

Compliance training through the use of verbal instructions and graduated guidance. The student is directed or instructed to perform the various individual overcorrection acts through verbal instructions and physical guidance of his limbs. The verbal instructions are given once and in a neutral tone of voice, as described previously.

TYPES OF OVERCORRECTION ACTS

There are several types of overcorrection acts that have been developed to deal with general classes of misbehavior, which will be discussed briefly here. A list of scientific studies that have employed these various types of overcorrection can be found in the Suggested Readings section at the end of this chapter.

Whenever a student is agitated and aggressive towards others or property, self-abuses, or creates a general commotion by screaming or making noise, the overcorrection rationale dictates that the student must compensate (overcorrect) by remaining quiet and relaxed for a prespecified period of time. As described previously (in the treatment of Robby's self-abuse by overcorrection), the procedure consists of requiring the student to lie quietly on a mat or bed until all signs of her agitation have disappeared. Once the student is quiet, she is required to complete any other overcorrection acts that were necessitated by her misbehavior. If the student becomes agitated or combative while she is performing these other overcorrection acts, she is once again required to lie down and become quiet. Thus, the consistent use of this procedure deters the student from using her agitation as a means of escaping the overcorrection. *This procedure is always the first overcorrection procedure delivered to agitated or disruptive students.*

Whenever the student's mouth comes into contact with potentially harmful substances, the logic of the overcorrection rationale dictates that this unhygienic oral contact be corrected by cleansing the student's mouth and lips with an oral antiseptic. Such oral-related misbehaviors might include biting oneself or others, chewing or mouthing objects, or eating inedible (nonnutritive) substances such as trash.

Whenever the student's misbehavior consists of stereotyped, repetitive acts such as self-stimulatory or self-abusive behaviors, the overcorrection rationale dictates that the student be required to move the body part used in the misbehavior only when instructed to do so rather than as a part of the repetitive act. This was seen in the treatment of Robby's self-abuse, when he was required to move his arms according to instructions.

EXAMPLES OF OVERCORRECTION PROGRAMS

In all instances where the student's misbehavior results in an environmental disruption, the overcorrection program should include both overcorrection components. The following examples illustrate misbehaviors that would receive the full overcorrection program of both components. The time required for each of the examples is usually 30 minutes, with equal amounts of time spent on each type of overcorrection act.

Scavenging. This behavior involves pica (the ingestion of nonnutritive substances such as trash, garbage, or cigarette butts) and coprophagy (the ingestion of fecal matter). The overcorrection procedure for coprophagy would consist of cleansing the mouth and hands to remove the fecal matter, and requiring the student to flush toilets and mop the area where the fecal matter was obtained. The same procedures would be used for pica except that the scavenger would be required to pick up and throw away trash (if trash had been eaten) or empty and clean ashtrays (if cigarette butts had been eaten) rather than flush toilets and mop.

Stripping (public disrobing). Let's say that an adolescent female student removed her clothing on the living unit. The overcorrection would require her to wear extra clothing and to improve the appearance of her classmates by buttoning or zipping unfastened clothing and/or combing their hair. If her normal attire consisted simply of a dress, bra, panties, and shoes, the overcorrection would require her to dress in panties, panty hose, a bra, a slip, a dress, and shoes.

Biting others. The overcorrection would consist of requiring that the biter lie on a mat or bed, then brush her teeth with an oral antiseptic, cleanse and medicate her victim's wound, apologize to everyone in the vicinity, and, finally, practice appropriate interactions.

Throwing objects. The overcorrection would require the student to lie on a mat, to straighten, pick up, and clean various objects in the room, especially those that are similar to the thrown object, and to apologize to everyone in the vicinity.

Toileting accidents. The overcorrection for wet pants would require the student to mop the floor where the accident occurred, wash her soiled clothing, dress herself in clean clothing, repeatedly walk to the toilet or potty chair, and rapidly engage in the entire chain of behaviors involved in proper toileting. The chain would be rapidly lowering the pants, sitting briefly on the toilet, and then rapidly raising the pants.

When no environmental disruption is created by the misbehavior, the only overcorrection component used is the one that requires repeated practice of appropriate behaviors in the situations in which the misbehavior normally occurs. Since self-stimulatory behaviors usually have no effect in the environment (the exceptions are mouthing and self-abuse if they are included under the general class of self-stimulatory behaviors), only the practice component is used to treat them. It's important to note that although self-stimulating students are not harming themselves or disturbing the environment, scientific studies have shown that they can't learn while they are self-stimulating. This is why we must take steps to reduce high rates of self-stimulatory behavior. A specific type of overcorrection practice is designed for each type of self-stimulatory behavior so that the body part that is used in the self-stimulation is brought under instructional control, that is, the student moves that body part when instructed to do so. The following examples illustrate the use of overcorrection with various forms of self-stimulatory behavior.

Head-weaving. When the student randomly moves his head from side to side, the overcorrection procedure would be conducted as follows. Immediately following a head-weave, the student's head would be gently restrained by the teacher. Once the student's head was still, the teacher would instruct the student to move his head in one of three positions, up, down, or straight. If the student did not immediately move his head in the instructed direction, the teacher would use graduated guidance to guide the student's head in that direction. The student would be required to hold each position for 15 seconds, after which another instruction would be given. Shadowing would be used whenever the student voluntarily moved his head in the instructed direction. The entire sequence might last 15 to 20 minutes. (The length of the overcorrection would ultimately be shortened and then eliminated, as was done with Robby, the self-abuser.)

Rocking while seated in a chair. Body rocking would be treated as follows. The rocker would be required to move his upper torso forward in the chair and to hold that position for 15 seconds and then to move his torso back in contact with the chair for 15 seconds. These alternating movements would be conducted until 20 minutes had elapsed since the student rocked. The rocker's shoulders would be guided whenever he didn't respond within 1 to 2 seconds to the instruction to move his torso.

Hand-flapping, hand-gazing, and paper-flipping. The student would be required to engage in the same overcorrection arm movements that were used with Robby, the self-abuser.

It's appropriate at this time to address two common misconceptions about the practicing of appropriate behaviors during overcorrection. The first is that positive reinforcers are given since the behaviors being practiced are appropriate. As mentioned previously, positive reinforcement is *never* given during the practice; otherwise the student might begin misbehaving in order to receive overcorrection. The second misconception is that this repeated practice is similar to negative practice (Chapter 3). Actually, the two procedures are completely dissimilar. As you recall, in negative practice the student repeatedly practices the inappropriate behavior rather than the appropriate behavior, as is the case in the practice during overcorrection.

Practice Set 8B

Answer the following questions.

1. The major difference between manual guidance and graduated guidance is that with graduated guidance the amount of the instructor's physical guidance (hand pressure) is adjusted from m_____ to m_____, depending on the student's performance at that moment.

2. During full graduated guidance, the instructor keeps her hands in f_____ contact with the student's hands.

3. During partial graduated guidance, the instructor guides the student's hands with t_____ and f_____.

4. During s_____, the instructor keeps her hands within an inch of the student's hands.

5. All three parts of graduated guidance can be used within each overcorrection session. True or False

6. When the student resists the graduated guidance, the instructor uses just enough f_____ to counteract the student's resistance and then reduces and finally eliminates this f_____ as the student stops resisting.

7. Describe how overcorrection might be used for each of the misbehaviors listed:
   a. spitting
   b. breaking windows
   c. rumination
   d. clothes ripping
   e. self-abusive biting
   f. self-stimulatory clapping
   g. self-stimulatory object mouthing
8. Which of the following is not a characteristic of over-correction?
   a. The overcorrection acts are directly related to the misbehavior.
   b. The overcorrection is implemented immediately following the misbehavior.
   c. The overcorrection requires repeated practice of the misbehavior.
   d. The overcorrection acts are performed rapidly.
9. Which of the following is not a common element in overcorrection programs?
   a. timeout from positive reinforcement
   b. positive feedback
   c. compliance training
   d. verbal instructions delivered in a neutral tone of voice
   e. a verbal reprimand

Answers are found on pages 173 and 174.

OVERCORRECTION AS A STEP TOWARD NORMALIZATION

The rationale used in developing overcorrection was that the use of natural negative consequences would promote normalization because it would help close the gap between the behavior of retarded persons and ourselves. While traditional Type I and II behavioral punishment procedures are effective, they often employ artificial consequences and only teach the student what not to do. On the other hand, the overcorrection procedure was developed as a realistic punishment consequence (the first overcorrection component) and as a means of teaching the student what he should have done (the second overcorrection component).

Perhaps the best way of illustrating how normalization is enhanced by overcorrection (the use of realistic, natural negative consequences) is by the following real-world example. It illustrates how normal persons generally correct the specific effects of their own misbehavior.

Suppose that you go to a friend's house for a visit. He invites you in and you both go into the living room and sit on the couch. After a while he goes to the kitchen and prepares some drinks. He returns with the drinks and you resume the conversation. For some reason you act carelessly and spill your drink on the couch. Your behavior of spilling your drink on the couch is inappropriate. There are several behavioral rationales he could use in providing a consequence for your spilling behavior. If he followed a physical punishment rationale (Type I punishment) he would immediately move toward you and slap you. If he followed a timeout rationale, he would immediately escort you to another room that was devoid of any reinforcing stimuli, such as a closet or cellar. If he followed a physical restraint rationale, he would somehow restrict your movements either by tying you up or holding you down on the floor. If he followed a DRO (Differential Reinforcement of Other Behavior) rationale, he would wait for a period of time to elapse during which you didn't spill any more of the drink and then give you a reinforcer. If he followed an extinction rationale, he would ignore you while the liquid seeped into the couch. If he followed a negative practice rationale, he would require you to repeatedly spill more drinks on the couch. There are a number of other equally absurd examples.

Obviously none of these procedures would be used because you are a "normal" individual. You probably would not have waited for him to provide a consequence, since as soon as you spilled the drink you would have made a mad dash into the kitchen or bathroom, obtained a damp cloth, and returned to the couch where you would begin wiping up the spill. After you had wiped up as much of the spill as possible, you would have offered to have the couch cleaned, since some of the spill would probably have already stained the couch. It wouldn't be feasible just to clean the one cushion that had been stained, because it would then be much cleaner than the rest of the couch. Thus, you would be overcorrecting for having spilled a drink on one cushion of the couch, since the entire couch would be cleaned as a result of your accident.

In this example, it can be seen that normal people can and do engage in forms of "overcorrection." And this "overcorrection" often seems to be the most natural and normal way to correct our mistakes. Given that this is the way "normal" people behave, that same rationale fits nicely within a program designed to promote the normalization of retarded students. In other words, whenever possible we should attempt to use the same procedures or methods with our retarded students that we use with each other.

ADVANTAGES AND DISADVANTAGES
OF OVERCORRECTION

Overcorrection offers several advantages and disadvantages in treating misbehaviors. As a punishment procedure, it has the general advantages associated with all punishment procedures (see Chapter 6). Some of the specific advantages of overcorrection already have been described in detail in the Characteristics of Overcorrection Acts section. Briefly, the advantages are:

1. The procedure is directly related to the misbehavior.
2. The student directly experiences the effort normally required of others to correct the effects of her misbehavior.
3. The procedure constitutes an extinction trial because the student has little time to enjoy or be reinforced by the effects of her misbehavior.
4. It represents timeout from positive reinforcement.
5. The procedure consists of an annoying effort requirement.

There are disadvantages associated with overcorrection that are shared with all forms of punishment (see Chapter 6) and some disadvantages that are unique to it:

1. Overcorrection is a complex procedure. The subtlety of several of the procedural components, such as graduated guidance, and the fact that each overcorrection program is uniquely designed to treat a specific misbehavior increase the chances that overcorrection will be conducted incorrectly. Unlike some programs such as timeout that can often be implemented successfully by simply giving written instructions to staff members (although it's not a good idea), a successful overcorrection program requires that all staff members be individually trained in the procedures. (A model for a staff training and certification procedure can be found in *Toilet Training the Retarded*, listed in the Suggested Readings section at the end of this chapter.) The complexity

of overcorrection also requires that staff performance be monitored more frequently than in most other programs. As a result, not only is more staff time spent on the overcorrection program, but more of the professional, consultant, or administrator's time as well.

2. The length of time required and the fact that an instructor has to be present throughout the procedure can be counterproductive when the student's misbehavior occurs at high rates and/or when only a few staff are available to provide programming for several students. In such cases either additional staffing must be sought or an alternative reductive procedure must be chosen.

3. Overcorrection's physically intrusive nature makes it inappropriate for physically strong students who may react to the use of graduated guidance by becoming combative. In general, when more than two staff members are involved at one time in overcorrecting a student, the chances of injury to someone are greatly increased.

However, as mentioned previously, the amount of time that overcorrection requires and the requirement that a staff person be present to give overcorrection can be viewed as advantages, since these requirements reduce or eliminate arbitrary or punitive applications of the procedure. A major problem associated with several of the reductive behavioral procedures is that they require little effort from the staff. For example, exclusionary timeout requires few staff response requirements once the student has been timed out and therefore is sometimes used when no prespecified misbehavior has occurred. Overcorrection, however, requires a great deal of time and effort by the instructor. As a result, the instructor is not likely to use overcorrection unless the misbehavior has indeed occurred.

Overcorrection procedures can be used to decrease a wide range of misbehaviors. Part of the appeal of using overcorrection is that it permits individualized treatment because the instructor must design the overcorrection procedure to fit the specific misbehavior. This, of course, represents the ultimate in individualized programming and permits the instructor to be creative in designing behavioral programs. As is true for all inhibitory or reductive procedures, there will be situations and students that overcorrection will not be appropriate or useful for. However, when applicable, overcorrection can be regarded as an effective, humane, and long-lasting method of reducing problem behaviors.

THE LEAST RESTRICTIVE TREATMENT MODEL

We've now discussed 10 procedures that will decrease an undesirable behavior and have grouped them into three levels within the Least Restrictive Treatment Model. Level 1 procedures contain no aversive or intrusive properties, while Level 2 procedures do contain some aversive or intrusive properties. Although Level 2 procedures are not very restrictive of the student's rights, you still should obtain written approval from your administration and the student or her parents or guardian before using a Level 2 procedure. Level 3 procedures are quite aversive and intrusive. Their use requires written permission from the student or her parents, the administration, and the human rights committee.

Level 1	Level 2	Level 3
DRO (Differential Reinforcement of Other Behavior)	Negative practice (when manual guidance is not given)	Negative practice (when manual guidance is given)
DRA (Differential Reinforcement of Appropriate Behavior)	Extinction	Physical restraint
DRI (Differential Reinforcement of Incompatible Behavior)	Nonexclusionary timeout	Exclusionary timeout
Satiation		Overcorrection

SUMMARY

Overcorrection is a Type I punishment procedure in which the misbehaving student is required to overcorrect the environmental effects of his misbehavior and/or to practice appropriate forms of behavior in those situations in which the misbehavior commonly occurs. Overcorrection has two components, which can be combined or used singly. In one component, the student is required to correct the consequences of his misbehavior by restoring the disturbed situation to a vastly improved state. In the other component, the student is required to repeatedly practice appropriate behaviors in the situation in which he normally misbehaves.

Overcorrection acts are designed to have the following characteristics: (1) they are directly related to the misbehavior and the student directly experiences the effort normally required of others to correct the effects of his misbehavior, (2) they are implemented immediately, and (3) they are performed rapidly, using graduated guidance. Graduated guidance has three parts: full graduated guidance, partial graduated guidance, and shadowing. One or all parts may be used in any overcorrection session.

There are four common elements in all overcorrection programs: (1) the use of verbal reprimands, (2) a period of timeout from positive reinforcement, (3) short verbal instructions delivered only once in a neutral voice, and (4) compliance training through the use of verbal instructions and graduated guidance.

Two common misconceptions about overcorrection are that positive reinforcement is given for the appropriate behavior practiced and that negative practice is similar to overcorrection. Positive reinforcement is *never* given during overcorrection, so that students won't misbehave in order to receive the overcorrection procedure. Negative practice is the opposite of overcorrection in that an *inappropriate* behavior is practiced, rather than an appropriate behavior as in overcorrection.

The general advantages of overcorrection are those that it shares with all punishment procedures (see Chapter 6), while its specific advantages are that (1) it's directly related to the misbehavior, (2) the student experiences the effort normally required of others to correct his misbehavior, (3) it constitutes an extinction trial, (4) it represents timeout from positive reinforcement, and (5) it's an annoying effort requirement. The general disadvantages of overcorrection are those that it shares with all punishment procedures (see Chapter 6), while its specific disadvantages are that (1) it's complex, (2) it can be lengthy and requires a staff member's full participation, and (3) it's physically intrusive. Overcorrection is a Level 3 procedure in the Least Restrictive Treatment Model because it's a physically intrusive procedure.

SUGGESTED READINGS

Barnard, J. D., Christopherson, E. R., & Wolf, M. M. Parent-mediated treatment of children's self-injurious behavior using overcorrection. *Journal of Pediatric Psychology*, 1976, *2*, 56-61.

Epstein, L. H., Doke, L. A., Sajwaj, T. E., Sorrell, S., & Rimmer, B. Generality and side effects of overcorrection. *Journal of Applied Behavior Analysis*, 1974, *7*, 385-390.

Foxx, R. M. The use of overcorrection to eliminate the public disrobing (stripping) of retarded women. *Behaviour Research and Therapy*, 1976, *14*, 53-61.

Foxx, R. M. Attention training: The use of overcorrection avoidance to increase eye contact of autistic and retarded children. *Journal of Applied Behavior Analysis*, 1977, *10*, 489-499.

Foxx, R. M., & Azrin, N. H. Restitution: A method of eliminating aggressive-disruptive behavior of retarded and brain damaged patients. *Behaviour Research and Therapy*, 1972, *10*, 15-27.

Foxx, R. M., & Azrin, N. H. The elimination of autistic, self-stimulatory behavior by overcorrection. *Journal of Applied Behavior Analysis*, 1973, *6*, 1-14.

Foxx, R. M., & Martin, E. D. Treatment of scavenging behavior (coprophagy and pica) by overcorrection. *Behaviour Research and Therapy*, 1975, *13*, 153-162.

Review Set 8

 1. Overcorrection is a Type I p_____ procedure because it reduces the future probability of occurrence of a misbehavior.

 2. Overcorrection acts are designed to have the following characteristics and hence advantages: (a) they are d_____ related to the misbehavior and often require the student to expend an annoying amount of e_____, (b) they are implemented i_____, and (c) they are performed r_____.

 3. During overcorrection, the instructor's verbal instructions are given in a n_____ tone of voice.

 4. G_____ g_____ is the manual guidance procedure that is used to ensure that the student will perform the overcorrection acts.

 5. The three parts of graduated guidance are f_____ graduated guidance, p_____ graduated guidance, and s_____.

 6. The common elements in all overcorrection programs are (a) the use of a v_____ r_____, (b) a period of t_____ from positive reinforcement, (c) v_____ i_____ delivered in a neutral tone of voice, and (d) c_____ training.

 7. The repeated practice of behaviors that may be a part of overcorrection differs from negative practice in that the student is required to practice a_____ rather than inappropriate behaviors.

 8. No positive r_____ is given during overcorrection.

9. The specific disadvantages of overcorrection are (a) its
   c_____, (b) the length of t_____ and amount of
   staff participation it requires, and (c) its physically
   i_____ nature.

10. Overcorrection is a Level _____ procedure in the Least
    Restrictive Treatment Model.

The answers are on page 174.

CHAPTER 9

Baseline Measurement

In the preceding chapters you've learned several techniques for decreasing behaviors. We'll now be turning to ways of recording and measuring behaviors to determine if an intervention is necessary or if your reduction program is successful. In this chapter you'll see how to measure the natural occurrence of a behavior you want to decrease, using one of two methods, and how to decide when enough measurement has been conducted for the reduction program to begin.

Measurement of a naturally occurring behavior reveals its *operant level*.

> The operant level is a description of the frequency of behavior before the intervention begins.

An operant level tells you how often the behavior occurs before you attempt to decrease it. For instance, Mr. Secter would like to reduce Denise's toileting accidents, which appear to be for attention since Denise has independently toileted herself many times. Before beginning a program to reduce accidents, Mr. Secter must determine how many times Denise wets her pants each day. Mr. Secter will use this information to determine the effectiveness of his program by simply comparing the number of accidents per day prior to the reductive program versus the number during the program. The period of time (or days) during which Denise's accidents (behavior) are measured before the intervention is called the *baseline period*.

> A baseline is the period of time during which a behavior is observed and measured without any intervention.

113

Determining the operant level during a baseline condition provides an objective measurement of the behavior's occurrence and helps in evaluating the effectiveness of a reduction program. It's extremely important that we know how often the behavior occurs under natural conditions so that we can make intelligent decisions about how to decrease it. Otherwise we find ourselves using impressions or guesses concerning the student's behavior, rather than using objective records.

Often it will appear that a behavior occurs more often than it really does. For example, Mr. Thomas, the school administrator, is disturbed because every time he encounters Gordon, a student in Ms. Wilson's class, Gordon is picking his face with his fingernails. When Mr. Thomas sees Gordon picking he always tells him to stop. Mr. Thomas wants to eliminate this behavior, so he asks Ms. Wilson to conduct a 2-week baseline in order to determine Gordon's operant level of face picking. The baseline reveals that Gordon only picked his face once every 2 weeks, which corresponded to Mr. Thomas' visits to the classroom. Measuring the occurrence of the behavior (operant level) during a baseline demonstrated to Mr. Thomas that Gordon's face picking was not the problem he thought it was. Furthermore, it indicated to Mr. Thomas that he should analyze his own behavior in order to determine why his presence was associated with Gordon's face picking. (The probable answer was that it was Mr. Thomas' attention that was maintaining Gordon's face picking, since Gordon's classroom instructors had learned over time that Gordon wouldn't pick his face if they simply ignored the behavior.)

Determining the operant level during baseline also helps us to establish whether or not our program to reduce a misbehavior has been effective. Mr. Rose's objective was to reduce the number of times Willie pulled his pants down in class. When Mr. Rose tallied Willie's operant level of pulling his pants down, he found that Willie did so an average of 10 times per day. Mr. Rose then began a DRO program in which he reinforced Willie every 2 hours if his pants were not pulled down. One week into the DRO program, Mr. Rose's data revealed that Willie was still pulling his pants down an average of 10 times per day. Willie's behavior had not decreased during the DRO program. As a result, Mr. Rose knew he needed to reevaluate his DRO program before he attempted further programs for Willie.

TAKING A BASELINE

Determining an operant level of behavior by taking a baseline measurement can be accomplished in a variety of ways depending on the particular behavior you wish to measure. We'll consider two common ways: frequency counting and time sampling.

Frequency Counting

> Frequency counting is a recording method in which the number of times a behavior occurs during a specified period of time is tallied.

The first and most general method is *frequency counting*, in which you tally the number of times the behavior occurs during a specified period of time. Each time the behavior occurs, simply place a hatch mark (/) or check mark (✔) on a sheet of paper. For example, you may wish to determine how often your student, Mary Kelly, will throw her spoon during lunch.

Name: Mary Kelly
Behavior to Be Counted: Number of times Mary throws her spoon during lunch

Date	Number of Times Behavior Occurred	Recorder
February 11	✔ ✔	Spear
February 12	✔ ✔	Spear
February 13	✔ ✔ ✔ ✔ ✔	Spear
February 14	✔ ✔ ✔	Essex
February 15	✔ ✔ ✔	Spear

The baseline record reveals that Mary's operant level of spoon throwing ranged from two to five times per lunch and averaged three times.

Time Sampling

> Time sampling is a recording method in which the student is observed at fixed intervals for a specified period of time and the occurrence or absence of a behavior during each interval is recorded.

A second common method of determining the operant level is *time sampling*. In time sampling you simply observe the student at fixed intervals, such as every 5 minutes, for a specified period of time, such as 30 seconds, and then record whether or not the behavior occurred. The behavior can then be expressed as a percentage, that is, the number of instances or observations in which the behavior was observed divided by the number of observations, times 100.

$$\frac{\text{number of instances}}{\begin{array}{c}\text{number of possible}\\ \text{instances}\end{array}} \times 100 = \begin{array}{c}\text{percentage of time}\\ \text{behavior occurs}\end{array}$$

Thus, rather than counting each occurrence of the behavior, you simply determine the percentage of time the behavior occurs. Time sampling is especially useful when the operant level of the behavior is very high, such as with self-stimulatory behavior, or when you wish to measure a behavior that may go on for several seconds or minutes, such as screaming. The following examples illustrate the time sampling method of recording.

Billy Thomson appears to rock continuously throughout the day and his attendant has decided to determine his operant level of rocking during an hour period. The time sampling baseline record on August 1 shows that Billy was rocking in 76.9% of the observed intervals.

Name: Billy Thomson

Behavior to Be Measured: *Rocking.* Billy will be observed every 5 minutes for 15 seconds during a 1-hour period. A check mark indicates that he rocked at some time during the observation interval. A circle indicates that rocking did not occur during the observation interval.

Date: August 1   Recorded by: Ed Jones

Time	Rocking Occurred (✔)	No Rocking Occurred (0)
9:00	✔	
9:05	✔	
9:10	✔	
9:15	✔	
9:20	✔	
9:25		0
9:30	✔	
9:35	✔	
9:40		0
9:45		0
9:50	✔	
9:55	✔	
10:00	✔	
Total	10	3

Percentage of Time Rocking = 76.9% (10 ÷ 13 x 100)

Bobby James' teachers are interested in determining his operant level of screaming during an unstructured free play activity that lasts for 15 minutes. The time sampling baseline record on April 10 shows that Bobby was screaming during 75% of the observed intervals.

Name: Bobby James

Behavior to Be Measured: *Screaming*. Bobby will be observed every minute for 5 seconds during the 15-minute unstructured free play activity. A check mark indicates that he was screaming at some time during the observation interval. A circle indicates that Bobby did not scream during the observation interval.

Date: April 10		Recorded by: Harvey Martin
Time	Screaming Occurred (✔)	No Screaming Occurred (0)
9:00	✔	
9:01	✔	
9:02	✔	
9:03		0
9:04	✔	
9:05	✔	
9:06	✔	
9:07	✔	
9:08	✔	
9:09		0
9:10	✔	
9:11	✔	
9:12	✔	
9:13	✔	
9:14		0
9:15		0
Total	12	4

Percentage of Time Screaming = 75% (12 ÷ 16 x 100)

ENDING THE BASELINE CONDITION

How do you determine how long to conduct baseline recordings? Let's return to the baseline record of Mary Kelly's spoon throwing.

Name: Mary Kelly

Behavior to Be Counted: Number of times Mary throws her spoon during lunch

Date	Number of Times Behavior Occurred	Recorder
February 11	✓ ✓	Spear
February 12	✓ ✓	Spear
February 13	✓ ✓ ✓ ✓ ✓	Spear
February 14	✓ ✓ ✓	Essex
February 15	✓ ✓ ✓	Spear

The baseline record reveals that Mary's operant level of spoon throwing ranged from two to five times per lunch and averaged three times. Note that the recording was conducted for 5 days. The number of days was not chosen arbitrarily. Rather, the baseline was conducted until the operant level appeared to be stable and the number for the final baseline day was no lower than the number for the previous day.

How do you know when you have a stable baseline? The answer comes from deciding whether or not the baseline adequately shows the range (variability) of the behavior or reveals any consistent downward trend. Thus, we determine when to cease baseline recording by asking two questions. First, does the baseline adequately show the range (variability) of the behavior? If the answer is yes, then we ask the second question: is the final baseline data point (number) as high or higher than the data point from the previous baseline session or day?

Let's consider these two questions in regard to Mary's baseline.

Does the baseline adequately show the range of the behavior? In other words, was the baseline conducted over a long enough period of time to ensure that no drastic changes or fluctuations in the operant level occurred? Mary's operant level of spoon-throwing showed no drastic changes—she did not throw a spoon one time at lunch one day and nine times the following day. Rather, her spoon throwing ranged between two and five times. Thus, the answer to the first question would be "Yes, the baseline accurately shows the range of the measured behavior." Because the answer is yes, it's appropriate to ask the second question. However, if the answer is no, then recording must be continued until you can answer yes.

Is the final baseline data point as high or higher than the data point from the previous baseline session or day? Mary threw a spoon three times on the last day and three times on the previous day. Thus, the answer to the second question is also yes.

Since the answer to both questions is yes, baseline data no longer need to be recorded, and it's appropriate to begin a program to decrease Mary's spoon throwing. If the answer to either question had been no, baseline data would still have been collected until a yes could be given to both questions. Remember, don't pose the second question until the first is answered affirmatively.

As mentioned previously, determining the operant level by conducting a baseline condition helps you determine the effectiveness of a program to reduce a behavior, since the level of the behavior during the program can be compared to the level during baseline. When you want to decrease a behavior, then that behavior should be lower in the program condition than it was during baseline. If it is, we can say the program was effective. (How effective would be determined by the amount or degree of reduction.) However, if the baseline is terminated prematurely and the behavior is decreasing when the baseline is terminated, we have no sound way of evaluating whether or not the program is working. (In fact, it could be that no program was necessary.)

For example, a major error would have been made if the teacher had decided to begin a program to decrease Mary's spoon throwing after the fourth day of recording. Mary had decreased her spoon throwing from five times on February 13 to three times on February 14. Had the program decreased her spoon throwing to once on February 15, the argument could have been made that Mary was already beginning to decrease her spoon throwing independent of the program. As a result the teacher would never know whether or not the program was successful in decreasing spoon throwing or whether it simply coincided with the same day that Mary had decreased her spoon throwing. Because of this dilemma, the teacher would not be likely to use the program to reduce the spoon throwing of other students. In effect, Mary's teacher would have failed to ask the two questions that would tell whether or not she could terminate the baseline recording.

Let's return to the baseline record of Bobby James' screaming behavior during an unstructured free play activity. Before, we only saw Bobby's first day of baseline, whereas now we have a 5-day record.

Name: Bobby James

Behavior to Be Measured: *Percentage of time Bobby screams.* Bobby will be observed every minute for 5 seconds during the 15-minute unstructured free play activity each school day.

Date	Percent Screaming	Recorder
April 10	75	Martin
April 11	63	Martin
April 12	72	Bornstein
April 13	65	Martin
April 14	69	Bornstein

The 5-day baseline record revealed that Bobby's operant level of screaming ranged from 63 to 75% per day and averaged 68.8%. Is this baseline record sufficient to allow us to begin a program to decrease Bobby's screaming? The record shows that the baseline was stable, since it was conducted long enough to ensure that no drastic changes in the operant level occurred. Furthermore, the final baseline percentage was higher than the previous day. As a result, we can suspend baseline recording and begin Bobby's treatment program.

Practice Set 9

Answer the following questions for each case.

1. Name: Susan Brown

   Behavior to Be Counted: Number of times Susan attempts to scratch another student

Date	Number of Times Behavior Occurred	Recorder
May 7	✔ ✔ ✔	Shelton
May 8	✔ ✔ ✔ ✔ ✔	Stevens
May 9	✔ ✔ ✔ ✔ ✔	Stevens
May 10	✔ ✔ ✔	Stevens
May 11	✔ ✔ ✔ ✔	Shelton

   a. The baseline record reveals that Susan's operant level of attempted scratches ranged from _____ to _____ times per day and averaged _____ times per day.

   b. Was the baseline conducted long enough to ensure that no drastic changes in the operant level occurred?

   c. Was the final baseline data point as high or higher than the previous day?

   d. Are more baseline recordings required? Why or why not?

2. Name: Ross Hall
   Behavior to Be Counted: Number of times Ross spits at his instructors

Date	Number of Times Behavior Occurred	Recorder
October 21	/	Ansel
October 22	/ /	Springer
October 23	0	Kohrs
October 24	/ /	Kohrs
October 25	/ /	Springer
October 28	/	Kohrs

a. The baseline record reveals that Ross' operant level of spitting at his instructor ranged from _____ to _____ times per day and averaged _____ times per day.

b. Was the baseline conducted long enough to ensure that no drastic changes in the operant level occurred?

c. Was the final baseline data point as high or higher than the previous day?

d. Are more baseline recordings required? Why or why not?

3. Name: Eric LeRouge
   Behavior to Be Measured: *Eric's out-of-seat behavior.* Eric will be observed for 5 seconds every 5 minutes during a 1-hour period. A hatch mark indicates that he was out of his chair during the observation interval. A circle indicates that Eric was in his seat during the observation interval.

Date: August 19		Recorded by: Crystal Peters
Time	Out of Seat (/)	In Seat (0)
1:00	/	
1:05		0
1:10	/	
1:15	/	
1:20	/	
1:25		0
1:30		0
1:35		0
1:40	/	
1:45	/	
1:50	/	
1:55		0
Total	7	5

What percentage of the time was Eric out of his seat?

4. Name: Phil Hunter

Behavior to Be Measured: *Percentage of time Phil stays off task*. The task is coloring with a crayon. Phil will be observed every minute for 5 seconds during the 15-minute coloring session each school day.

Date	Percent Off Task	Recorder
November 12	39	Barnes
November 13	35	Barnes
November 14	36	Bornstein
November 15	40	Barnes
November 16	44	Bornstein

a. The baseline record revealed that Phil's operant level of being off task ranged from _____ to _____% per day and averaged _____%.

b. Was the baseline conducted long enough to ensure that no drastic changes in the operant level occurred?

c. Was the final baseline percentage as high or higher than the previous day?

d. Are more baseline data required? Why or why not?

5. Name: Pat Stephens

Behavior to Be Measured: *Percentage of time Pat is flicking her fingers*. Pat will be observed for 10 seconds every 5 minutes throughout the 6-hour school day and her percentage of finger flicking will be calculated for each hourly session.

Date: December 2

Hour Number	Percent of Finger Flicking	Recorder
1	14	Smithwick
2	36	Smithwick
3	70	Rambo
4	19	Littlejohn
5	61	Rambo
6	17	Littlejohn

a. The baseline record reveals that Pat's percentage of finger flicking behavior ranged from _____ to _____% per session and averaged _____%.

b. Was the baseline conducted long enough to ensure that no drastic changes in the operant level occurred?

c. Was the final baseline session percentage as high or higher than the previous session?

d. Are more baseline data required? Why or why not?

Answers are found on pages 174 and 175.

SUMMARY

The operant level describes the occurrence of the behavior before a reductive program begins. It is determined by taking a baseline, which is the period of time during which a behavior is observed and measured prior to the intervention. Determining the operant level during a baseline condition permits the objective measurement of the occurrence of a behavior and helps in evaluating a program's effectiveness.

Two methods of taking baseline measurements are *frequency counting*, which consists of tallying the number of times the behavior occurs during a specified period of time, and *time sampling*, which consists of recording whether or not the behavior occurred during a specified period.

To determine whether or not an adequate baseline has been established so that you can begin a program to reduce the behavior, consider the following questions: (1) Does the baseline adequately show the range (variability) of the behavior? (2) Is the final baseline data point as high or higher than the data point from the previous baseline session or day? When sufficient baseline data have been collected so both questions can be answered yes, the intervention can begin.

SUGGESTED READINGS

Craighead, W. E., Kazdin, A. E., & Mahoney, M. J. *Behavior modification: Principles, issues and applications.* Boston: Houghton-Mifflin, 1976.

Gambrill, E. D. (Ed.). *Behavior modification: Handbook of assessment, intervention and evaluation.* San Francisco: Jossey-Bass, 1977.

Thompson, T. I., & Grabowski, J. (Eds.). *Behavior modification of the mentally retarded.* New York: Oxford University Press, 1972.

Review Set 9

1. The o_____ l_____ describes the occurrence of the behavior before the intervention begins.

2. A b_____ is the period of time during which a behavior is observed and measured before the intervention begins.

3. Determining the operant level via a baseline allows the o_____ measurement of a behavior's occurrence and helps in evaluating the effectiveness of the program.

4. One method of determining an operant level is to t_____ the number of times the behavior occurs. This method is called f_____ counting.

5. Another method of determining an operant level is t_____ s_____, in which you record whether or not the behavior occurred during a specified period.

6. The two questions you must ask to determine whether you have collected sufficient baseline data are: (1) Does the baseline adequately show the r_____ (variability) of the behavior? and (2) Is the final baseline d_____ p_____ as high or higher than the previous data point?

The answers are on page 175.

CHAPTER 10

Program Measurement
and Evaluation

In this chapter we'll tell you how to measure and evaluate your program's success. Several issues will be considered: measuring the reliability of the behavioral recording, using two methods to record the behaviors during the intervention, and determining by graphs and criterion levels whether a program is working or not.

In the previous chapter we briefly discussed the critical role of observing behaviors. You learned that to determine the student's operant level, or behavior prior to the intervention, it was necessary to record the behavior during a baseline period. As you now know, the baseline (1) allows the objective measurement of the occurrence of a behavior, and (2) helps you determine the effectiveness of a program after the intervention begins by comparing the baseline level of behavior to the level after the intervention. If the behavior has decreased substantially during the intervention, the program has been effective. The best way to determine the effectiveness of a program is to set a criterion level for success before beginning treatment.

Let's reconsider frequency counting and time sampling, this time to see how these two recording methods can be used during an intervention to objectively determine when a program is not working. (Note: There are a number of ways of recording behaviors besides the two already discussed. For more information, consult the suggested readings at the end of this and the previous chapter.)

FREQUENCY COUNTING

Frequency counting was introduced in the previous chapter as a procedure in which you count the number of times a specific behavior occurs within a set period of time. For example, Ms. McFadden has been working with Ann, a student in her class who hits other students. Before beginning an intervention to decrease Ann's hitting, Ms. McFadden must conduct a baseline to determine how often it occurs. Since Ann's hitting behaviors are discrete and countable events, Ms. McFadden decides to use the frequency counting method. Specifically, she's interested in knowing the number of times Ann hits other students.

Obtaining Reliable Records

One concern that Ms. McFadden had was that there would be times when she would be out of the classroom with another student, and her aide, Ms. Cramer, would be responsible for recording whether or not Ann had hit someone. Ms. McFadden wasn't concerned about whether or not Ms. Cramer would do the recording but rather whether or not she and Ms. Cramer would observe and record hitting in the same way. The problem was that Ann not only hit other students but also would lightly tap them with her hands. Both behaviors looked highly similar, the major difference being the impact of Ann's hand. Ms. McFadden wondered whether Ms. Cramer would record a tap as a hit, since only hits were to be recorded and treated. They had discussed how they would define and thereby record Ann's hitting; still, Ms. McFadden could not be sure they both agreed on exactly what constituted a hit. In addition, Ms. McFadden knew that Ann was Ms. Cramer's favorite student and that Ms. Cramer wanted Ann to do well and disliked having to use negative consequences with her. As a result, Ms. McFadden was somewhat concerned that Ms. Cramer might give Ann the "benefit of the doubt" on whether or not she had hit someone. This issue bothered Ms. McFadden, since she wanted the treatment program to be applied consistently by both of them in order to eliminate Ann's hitting.

In behavioral terms, Ms. McFadden's problem concerned whether or not there would be *interobserver reliability* or agreement regarding Ann's hitting.

> Interobserver reliability is a measure of the degree to which two or more observers agree that a specific behavior occurred.

Interobserver reliability is an important concern because it's extremely rare that a single individual records and conducts a student's program. As a result, it's important that everyone responsible for recording or conducting the program agree that the misbehavior occurred. Otherwise instances of the misbehavior may be missed by some individuals or an intervention may be applied when in fact the misbehavior did not occur. Lack of interobserver reliability is especially crucial when the misbehavior is (1) highly disruptive or dangerous to others, or (2) being treated by a highly aversive procedure. In the former case, lack of agreement could lead to a staff member failing to provide a consequence, thereby setting up a situation where the misbehavior is reinforced intermittently and thus strengthened. (Each time we fail to provide the consequence, the behavior is likely to be reinforced. Or, in the case of extinction, the misbehavior is strengthened when we fail to ignore it.) In the latter case, this lack of agreement is unfair to the student because it means she could receive the aversive procedure when, in fact, she had not misbehaved.

Calculating Reliability

In calculating reliability we're interested in determining whether two or more persons who are observing a student agree that a specific behavior occurred. Continuing with our example, Ms. McFadden decided to determine interobserver reliability between herself and Ms. Cramer. To do so, they both observed Ann for a day during the baseline and independently recorded her hitting. (They did not look at each other's records until the end of the day.) In order to synchronize their records, they divided the recording sheet into 15-minute intervals of time.

At the end of the day their records were as shown.

Recorder: McFadden	Type of Recording: Frequency	Recorder: Cramer	Type of Recording: Frequency
Student: Ann		Student: Ann	
Behavior: Hitting other students	Date: August 10	Behavior: Hitting other students	Date: August 10
Condition: Baseline		Condition: Baseline	
Time	Behavior Occurred	Time	Behavior Occurred
9:00-9:15		9:00-9:15	
9:15-9:30		9:15-9:30	

Time	Behavior Occurred	Time	Behavior Occurred
9:30-9:45	/	9:30-9:45	/
9:45-10:00		9:45-10:00	
10:00-10:15		10:00-10:15	
10:15-10:30		10:15-10:30	
10:30-10:45		10:30-10:45	
10:45-11:00		10:45-11:00	
11:00-11:15	/	11:00-11:15	/
11:15-11:30		11:15-11:30	
11:30-11:45	/	11:30-11:45	/
11:45-12:00		11:45-12:00	
12:00-12:15		12:00-12:15	
12:15-12:30		12:15-12:30	
12:30-12:45	/	12:30-12:45	/
12:45-1:00		12:45-1:00	
1:00-1:15		1:00-1:15	
1:15-1:30		1:15-1:30	
1:30-1:45	/	1:30-1:45	/
1:45-2:00	/	1:45-2:00	
2:00-2:15	/	2:00-2:15	/
2:15-2:30		2:15-2:30	
2:30-2:45		2:30-2:45	
2:45-3:00		2:45-3:00	
Total	7	Total	6

One way of calculating interobserver reliability or the percentage of agreement between the observers is to use this formula:

$$\text{interobserver reliability} = \frac{\text{number of times observers agreed}}{\text{number of times observers agreed} + \text{number of times observers disagreed}} \times 100 = \text{percentage of agreement}$$

Using this formula we can calculate the agreement (interobserver reliability) between Ms. McFadden and Ms. Cramer on the number of times Ann hit others on August 10. First we must determine the number of times they agreed and disagreed. Looking at their recording sheets we see that they agreed that Ann hit someone between 9:30-9:45, 11:00-11:15, 11:30-11:45, 12:30-12:45, 1:30-1:45, and 2:00-2:15, and disagreed between 1:45-2:00 in that Ms. McFadden saw Ann hit someone, whereas Ms. Cramer did not. Thus, the two agreed in six instances and disagreed on one. Using the formula we calculate that their percentage of agreement or reliability score is 85.7%.

$$\text{interobserver reliability} = \frac{6}{6 + 1} \times 100 = 85.7\%$$

A second way to determine reliability when frequency data are recorded is to divide the lower number by the higher number and multiply the result by 100. In this case, Ms. Cramer had the lower number of recorded hits, six, while Ms. McFadden had the higher number, seven. Dividing 6 by 7 and multiplying by 100, we find that their reliability score is again 85.7%. (There are a number of ways to calculate interobserver reliability and some of these methods are quite sophisticated. Interested readers can find a more comprehensive treatment of the topic in some of the publications listed at the end of the chapter.)

In general, the minimum percentage of interobserver reliability you should accept is above 70% and preferably above 80%. In this case, the two instructors can feel fairly confident that they are both in agreement as to when Ann hits someone because they agreed on 85.7% of the instances that occurred.

Recording and Evaluating the Baseline and Intervention

Having obtained a satisfactory percentage of interobserver reliability, the instructors continued the baseline recordings of Ann's hitting. The following chart summarizes Ann's 5-day baseline record.

Student: Ann   Type of Recording: Frequency
Behavior: Hitting other students
Condition: Baseline

Date	Time	Number of Times Behavior Occurred	Recorder
August 10	9 a.m.-3 p.m.	卌 //	McFadden
August 11	9 a.m.-3 p.m.	卌 //	McFadden
August 12	9 a.m.-3 p.m.	卌 //	Cramer
August 13	9 a.m.-3 p.m.	卌	McFadden
August 14	9 a.m.-3 p.m.	卌 ////	Cramer

The baseline revealed that Ann's hitting averaged seven times per day and ranged from five to nine times. Ms. McFadden decided to discontinue the baseline condition and begin the intervention program because the baseline was stable and the last data point was higher than the one for the previous day (see Chapter 9). She would conduct another interobserver reliability check during the intervention program. To evaluate the success of the intervention program, Ms. McFadden set the following

criterion level: after 5 days the intervention will decrease Ann's
hitting by 70% below the baseline average.

The intervention condition consisted of placing Ann in a
timeout room for 5 minutes whenever she hit or attempted to hit
someone. The frequency data collected for the first 2 weeks of the
timeout room intervention follow.

Student: Ann   Type of Recording: Frequency
Behavior: Hitting other students
Condition: Five minutes of timeout
  in the timeout room

Date	Time	Number of Times Behavior Occurred	Recorder
August 17	9 a.m.-3 p.m.	~~////~~ //	McFadden
August 18	9 a.m.-3 p.m.	///	Cramer
August 19	9 a.m.-3 p.m.	////	Cramer
August 20	9 a.m.-3 p.m.	//	McFadden
August 21	9 a.m.-3 p.m.	/	Cramer
August 24	9 a.m.-3 p.m.	0	Cramer
August 25	9 a.m.-3 p.m.	/	McFadden
August 26	9 a.m.-3 p.m.	0	McFadden
August 27	9 a.m.-3 p.m.	0	McFadden
August 28	9 a.m.-3 p.m.	0	Cramer

Ms. McFadden decided to graph Ann's baseline and treatment
records because it would offer her a visual representation of how
well the timeout program was working.

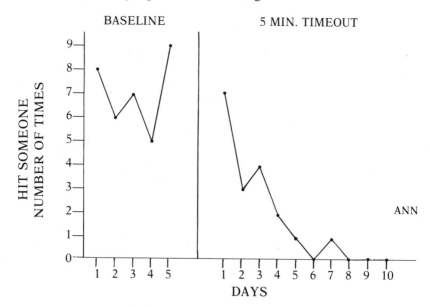

After comparing the records (Ann's frequency of hitting) before and after the timeout intervention, Ms. McFadden was pleased to see that the timeout was indeed successfully decreasing Ann's hitting beyond the 70% criterion level for success. The timeout decreased Ann's hitting by 86% within 5 days (on the fifth day of treatment Ann only hit once, which was an 86% reduction from the baseline average of seven times per day). As a result, she continued the timeout program for 2 more weeks and eliminated Ann's hitting.

You can see how much easier it is to determine whether a procedure is working when you look at a graph versus a recording sheet. Even before the percentage decrease was calculated, the graph very quickly and clearly shows that Ann's hitting behavior decreased steadily during the timeout treatment program. It's a good idea to graph the baseline and treatment records for each misbehavior you treat. Doing so will enable you to make better decisions concerning the effectiveness of your treatment program. Also, a graph is easily and quickly understood by parents, administrators, other staff, and human rights committees.

Let's look at another example of frequency counting. Barbara, another student in Ms. McFadden's room, would run out of the classroom. After 6 days of baseline recording, Ms. McFadden began working on Barbara's running out of the classroom behavior. She selected a DRO program as the intervention and set the criterion level of success as a 70% reduction from baseline after 5 days. Her baseline data indicated that Barbara ran out of the classroom an average of six times per day or once every hour. Accordingly, Ms. McFadden decided to schedule a 30-minute DRO interval in which Barbara would be reinforced at the end of each 30-minute period in which she had not attempted to run away (see Chapter 2 for a full description of DRO).

Here is a graph that shows Barbara's running out of the classroom during the baseline and through 1 week of the 30-minute DRO procedure.

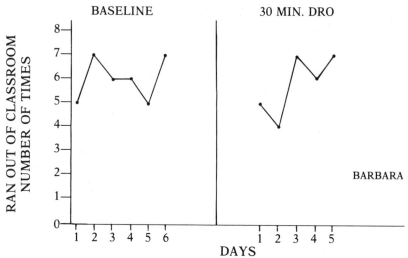

The graph shows that the 30-minute DRO program had very little, if any, effect on Barbara's running away, since there was little difference between her frequency of running away before or during treatment. Her baseline average of running away was 6 times per day and her average during the DRO program was 5.8 times per day. Thus, the criterion level for success was not achieved. As a result, Ms. McFadden decided to add a timeout procedure to the DRO program. In the timeout program, Barbara would be required to spend 5 minutes in the timeout room whenever she attempted to run out of the classroom. After Ms. McFadden had conducted the combined program for 5 days, the graph looked as shown.

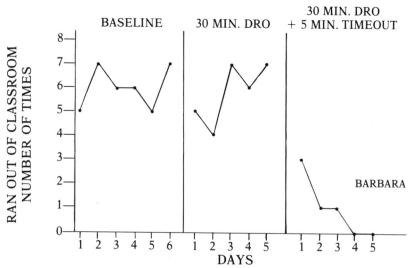

The graph shows clearly that the addition of the timeout room intervention produced a rapid decrease in Barbara's running away. During the 5 days that the timeout program was in effect, Barbara's running away averaged only once per day. Thus, the addition of the timeout procedure reduced Barbara's running away by 83.3% relative to the baseline, achieving the criterion level of success. (The baseline average was 6 times per day, timeout average was 1 time per day, 5/6 x 100 = 83.3% reduction from baseline.) As a result, Ms. McFadden continued to use the timeout program until Barbara's running away was eliminated.

Again, you can see how helpful it is to graph your program data or records. When records are graphed, it's immediately apparent whether or not an intervention is working. If your graph shows that it isn't, either add a more restrictive intervention to the existing program or discontinue the existing program and either examine it for problems and revise it or institute a more powerful (restrictive) procedure.

Practice Set 10A

Barbara also hit her instructors and would pull her classmates' hair. Here are the programs that Ms. McFadden instituted to treat Barbara's hitting and hair pulling. A 5-minute timeout room program was used to treat both misbehaviors because it had been used effectively to eliminate Barbara's running away. For both misbehaviors, the criterion level for success was a 60% reduction below baseline after 10 days.

After 2 weeks of treatment, the graph for hitting the teachers looked like this.

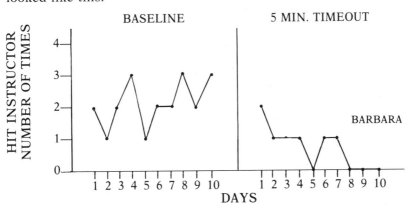

Answer the following questions.

1. Was the baseline assessment adequate? Why?

2. Was the timeout procedure effective?
3. What was the baseline daily average for hitting? The treatment daily average?
4. By what percent was hitting reduced in the treatment phase?
5. Was the criterion level for success achieved?

After 2 weeks of treatment, Barbara's graph for hair pulling looked like this.

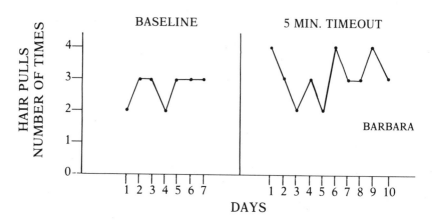

Answer the following questions.

6. Was the baseline assessment adequate?
7. What was the baseline daily average of hair pulling? The treatment daily average?
8. Was the timeout procedure effective?
9. What should Ms. McFadden do?

Answers are found on pages 175 and 176.

TIME SAMPLING

Time sampling was introduced in the previous chapter as a procedure in which you observe the student at fixed intervals for a specified period of time and then record whether or not the behavior occurred. The behavior can then be expressed as a percentage of the total number of observation intervals.

Ms. Cody would like to reduce Jane's eye poking. Jane is a blind student who pokes her eye with her fingers because it stimulates the optic nerve and she "sees" light flashes. Jane is currently wearing a specially designed football helmet with a face mask to prevent her from touching her eyes. Due to the serious nature of

Jane's behavior, Ms. Cody will conduct as brief a baseline as possible, since she must remove Jane's helmet in order to measure eye poking. She'll also determine interobserver reliability once during the baseline and once during the treatment.

During the baseline, Jane will be observed every 10 seconds for 2 minutes. Thus, there will be a total of 12 observations each time. Interobserver reliability between Ms. Cody and her aide, Mr. Monroe, will be conducted during the first baseline observation session. At the end of the session their records look as follows.

Recorder: Cody	Recorder: Monroe
Student: Jane	Student: Jane
Behavior: Eye poking	Behavior: Eye poking
Condition: Baseline	Condition: Baseline
Type of Recording: Time sampling	Type of Recording: Time sampling
Date: June 8	Date: June 8

Seconds

10	20	30	40	50	60
✓		✓	✓		✓
✓	✓	✓	✓	✓	✓

Total Observation Intervals   12
Total Observation Intervals in
  Which Behavior Occurred   10
Percentage of Time
  Eye Poking   83.3%

Seconds

10	20	30	40	50	60
✓		✓	✓	✓	✓
✓	✓	✓	✓	✓	✓

Total Observation Intervals   12
Total Observation Intervals in
  Which Behavior Occurred   11
Percentage of Time
  Eye Poking   91.7%

As noted before, to calculate interobserver reliability we must first determine the number of times the observers agreed and disagreed. Inspecting the baseline record, we find that they agreed in every observation interval except the fifth interval in Minute 1. We'll exclude those observation intervals in which neither observer reported seeing the behavior occur, in this case, the second observation interval of Minute 1. Thus, the two observers agreed on 10 instances and disagreed on 1. Using the interobserver reliability formula we can calculate their percentage of agreement or reliability score:

$$\text{interobserver reliability} = \frac{10}{10 + 1} \times 100 = 90.9\%$$

Having obtained a satisfactory interobserver reliability score, Ms. Cody continued the baseline recordings of Jane's eye poking. A summary of Jane's baseline record follows. All baseline sessions were conducted on June 8.

Student: Jane   Type of Recording: Time sampling
Behavior: Eye poking
Condition: Baseline

	Number of Intervals (10 sec.) in Which Behavior Was Observed	Total Number of Observation Intervals	Percentage of Time Behavior Occurred	Recorder
Session 1	10	12	83.3	Cody
Session 2	9	12	75	Monroe
Session 3	10	12	83.3	Monroe
Session 4	11	12	91.7	Cody

Average Percentage of Time 83.3%

The brief four-session baseline (four 2-minute observation sessions) showed that Jane was poking her eye in an average of 83.3% of the intervals. Because the baseline had been conducted for a sufficient period, Ms. Cody began her first intervention procedure. She had designed two levels of intervention. Her first treatment consisted of a DRI procedure in which Jane would be reinforced every 3 seconds for squeezing a Nerf ball with both hands. Squeezing the ball was selected because it was incompatible with eye poking and provided Jane with sensory stimulation and an appropriate motor response. The second treatment would consist of manually restraining Jane's hands at her sides for 1 minute whenever she attempted to poke her eye. This behavioral physical restraint procedure would be combined with the DRI procedure. (Of course, the second treatment was more aversive, a Level 3 procedure in the Least Restrictive Treatment Model.) Ms. Cody's criterion for deciding to institute the second treatment was if the DRI procedure failed to reduce eye poking to below 50% after five treatment sessions (a 30% reduction from baseline). There is no standard practice for deciding what criterion level to choose. However, a good ball park figure is a 30% reduction within 1 week or after five treatment sessions. Each session of this second treatment would still be 2 minutes in length.

The treatment records for the first five sessions of the 3-second DRI procedure are shown here.

Student: Jane   Type of Recording: Time sampling
Behavior: Eye poking
Condition: DRI 3 seconds
Date: June 9

	Number of Intervals (10 sec.) in Which Behavior Was Observed	Total Number of Observation Intervals	Percentage of Time Behavior Occurred	Recorder
Session 1	9	12	75	Cody
Session 2	8	12	66.7	Monroe
Session 3	9	12	75	Cody
Session 4	9	12	75	Cody
Session 5	8	12	66.7	Monroe

Average Percentage of Time 71.7%

The graph displaying the treatment records for the five sessions of the DRI procedure follows. (All five sessions were conducted on June 9.)

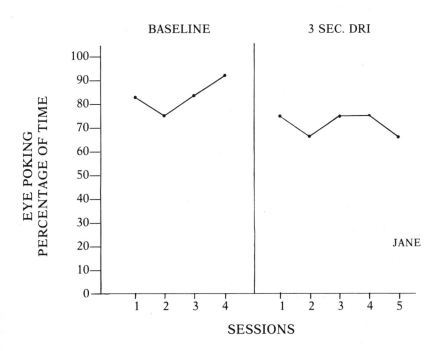

The graph shows that Jane's eye poking averaged 71.7% during the five sessions that the 3-second DRI procedure was in effect. Since the DRI procedure had not reduced Jane's eye poking to below 50% of the time (or a 30% reduction from baseline), Ms. Cody was justified in instituting the physical restraint procedure. To avoid biasing the treatment records, she would extend the length of each session to 12 minutes. The records could be biased if the session length remained at 2 minutes because during the 1-minute physical restraint procedure Jane wouldn't have the opportunity to eye poke. As a result, the records would show that Jane had not eye poked for six 10-second observation intervals or 1 minute. This, of course, would artificially inflate the treatment effect. An example of how this biasing could occur is illustrated here.

Seconds

	10	20	30	40	50	60
Minute 1	✓	PR	PR	PR	PR	PR
Minute 2	PR			✓	PR	PR

PR = Physical Restraint

As you can see, Jane would be physically restrained in eight of the twelve 10-second intervals. Thus, she would only have four opportunities or intervals in which to eye poke. Yet if we calculate the percentage of time eye poking occurred without considering the physical restraint intervals, we end up with eye poking being shown to occur only 50% of the time (two of four intervals). But is the physical restraint procedure really that effective? We can't say for sure. That's why the treatment sessions should be extended to 12 minutes in length so that Jane has the same number of opportunities to eye poke during the physical restraint plus DRI treatment condition that she had during the baseline and DRI conditions, that is, 12 opportunities because there were 12 observation intervals.

The rule for avoiding biasing is as follows: *the student should have at least the same number of opportunities each observation session to misbehave during treatment as during the baseline.* In this way the two conditions will be comparable and meaningful comparisons between them can be made. Therefore, when your reductive procedure lasts longer than an observation interval, such as a 30-second physical restraint procedure when observations are made every 10 seconds for a 1-minute period, you must extend the observation period so that the student has the opportunity to misbehave as much during the treatment as she did during the baseline. Thus, the 1-minute observation interval would be extended to 4 minutes, permitting the student the opportunity to misbehave six times and receive physical restraint six times, as shown in this chart.

		Seconds				
	10	20	30	40	50	60
Minute 1	✓	PR	PR	PR	✓	PR
Minute 2	PR	PR	✓	PR	PR	PR
Minute 3	✓	PR	PR	PR	✓	PR
Minute 4	PR	PR	✓	PR	PR	PR

The treatment records for the first five sessions of the combined 3-second DRI procedure and 1-minute physical restraint procedure are shown here.

Student: Jane   Type of Recording: Time sampling
Behavior: Eye poking
Condition: DRI 3 seconds and
    physical restraint 1 minute
Date: June 9

	Number of Intervals (10 sec.) in Which Behavior Was Observed	Total Number of Intervals	Percentage of Time Behavior Occurred	Number of Times Restraint Implemented	Recorder
Session 1	6	36	16.7	6	Monroe
Session 2	5	42	11.9	5	Cody
Session 3	6	36	16.7	6	Monroe
Session 4	3	54	5.5	3	Monroe
Session 5	0	72	0	0	Cody

Average Percentage of Time 10.2%

Note that the treatment sessions differed in the number of total intervals because 60 seconds (or six 10-second intervals) were subtracted each time the physical restraint was implemented. For example, in Session 2 the physical restraint was implemented five times or for 5 minutes (thirty 10-second observation intervals), which means that 30 intervals were subtracted from the 72 that were possible (12 minutes of 10-second intervals = 72 intervals).

Thus, the 5 intervals in which the eye poking was observed were divided by 42 intervals (the number of intervals in which Jane had the opportunity to eye poke) in order to determine her percentage of eye poking in Session 2.

In Session 4, interobserver reliability was assessed. Both observers, Cody and Monroe, observed Jane to eye poke in the same three intervals, thereby yielding a perfect 100% score.

After five 12-minute sessions of the combined 3-second DRI procedure and 1-minute physical restraint procedure, Jane's graph looked as follows.

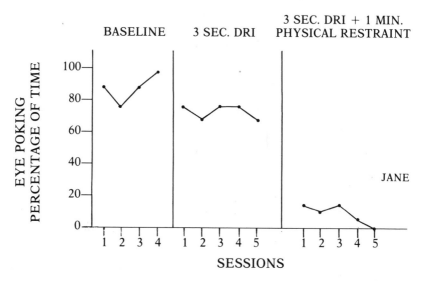

The graph shows clearly that the addition of the physical restraint procedure produced a rapid decrease in Jane's eye poking. During the five sessions of DRI plus physical restraint, Jane's eye poking averaged 10.2% versus 83.3% and 71.7% in the respective baseline and DRI-alone conditions. Thus, the combined procedure decreased Jane's eye poking from baseline by 87.8% ($83.3 - 10.2 = 73.1; 73.1 \div 83.3 \times 100 = 87.8\%$) and from the DRI-alone condition by 85.8%. After three additional sessions, eye poking was eliminated. At that point, Ms. Cody extended the duration of the treatment sessions to 30 minutes and conducted three sessions per day.

Practice Set 10B

After inspecting each graph, answer the questions.

1.

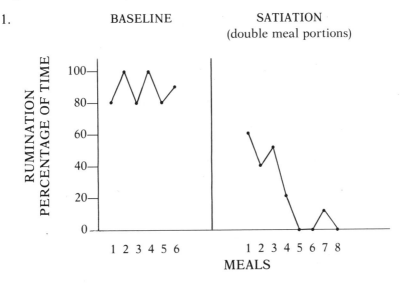

BASELINE

SATIATION
(double meal portions)

MEALS

a. Was the baseline assessment adequate?
b. Was the satiation procedure effective?

2.

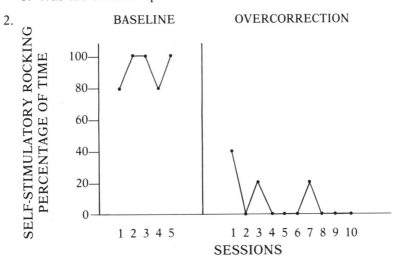

BASELINE

OVERCORRECTION

SESSIONS

a. What was the baseline average for rocking?
b. What was the treatment average for rocking?

Answer the following questions.

3. Two child care workers were attempting to measure inter-observer reliability. Their recording sheets looked as follows.

	Observer 1 Seconds

	10	20	30	40	50	60
Minute 1	✔		✔		✔	
Minute 2	✔		✔		✔	
Minute 3	✔		✔			✔

	Observer 2 Seconds

	10	20	30	40	50	60
Minute 1	✔		✔			
Minute 2	✔	✔			✔	
Minute 3	✔					✔

   a. What was their interobserver reliability score?
   b. What percentage of the time did each observer record that
       the behavior occurred?
4. Ms. Campbell is using a 30-second overcorrection procedure
   to treat Earl's hand-flapping during 5-minute treatment sessions. The overcorrection procedure consists of Ms. Campbell guiding Earl's hands into various positions. As a result,
   Earl has no opportunity to hand flap during the overcorrection. Here is Earl's recording sheet for the first session of
   treatment.

Seconds

	10	20	30	40	50	60
Minute 1	✔	OC	OC	OC		✔
Minute 2	OC	OC	OC			
Minute 3	✔	OC	OC	OC	✔	OC
Minute 4	OC	OC			✔	OC
Minute 5	OC	OC	✔	OC	OC	OC

OC = Overcorrection

   Based on the number of opportunities he had, what was
   Earl's percentage of hand-flapping during the session?
5. Ms. Aaronoff is treating Barney for ear scratching. She has
   designed two procedures. The first and least restrictive consists of a 15-second DRI procedure. The second and more
   restrictive is a 2-minute physical restraint procedure. If the
   DRI procedure doesn't reduce Barney's ear scratching to
   below 40% of his baseline average after five sessions, Ms.
   Aaronoff will implement the physical restraint procedure.
   Here is the graph showing the baseline and five sessions of
   the DRI program.

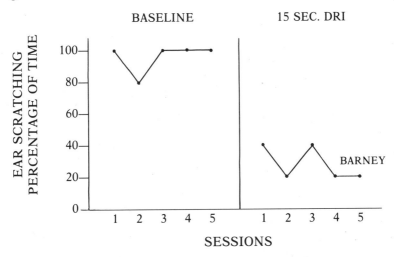

SESSIONS

a. What was the baseline average of ear scratching?
b. What was the average for ear scratching during the DRI condition?
c. During the DRI procedure, what was the percentage reduction from baseline?
d. Should Ms. Aaronoff continue the DRI procedure or institute the physical restraint procedure?

Answers are found on page 176.

SUMMARY

In order to evaluate the success of a program you must have an adequate baseline, an acceptable level of interobserver reliability in the baseline and treatment conditions, and a criterion level of success by which the treatment procedure will be judged.

Before recording data, observers need to agree on exactly which behaviors are to be counted or measured. Interobserver reliability is the measure of the degree to which two or more observers agree that a specific behavior occurred. Determining reliability is important for ensuring that records are accurate and occurrences of the behavior are properly treated, especially when the misbehavior is highly disruptive or is being treated with a highly aversive procedure. Interobserver reliability is calculated by either dividing the number of times observers agreed by the number of times they agreed plus disagreed, or dividing the lower number by the higher, and multiplying by 100.

This gives the percentage of agreement between observers. The minimum acceptable percentage is above 70%, and it is preferable to have it above 80%.

A treatment procedure to decrease a behavior is evaluated by comparing the level of behavior during treatment to its baseline level. To avoid biasing time sampling records when the procedure lasts longer than one observation interval, you must be sure to lengthen the observation time to afford the student the same number of opportunities to misbehave during the intervention as were present during the baseline. A graph provides a quick and easy visual way of determining the effectiveness of a procedure; but to follow the Least Restrictive Treatment Model, you must also set a criterion level of behavior reduction by which each procedure will be judged. This criterion level is usually a minimum percentage by which the behavior must be decreased within a specified number of days or sessions. If the procedure fails to meet the criterion level, then it should be revised or a more restrictive procedure should be added or substituted.

SUGGESTED READINGS

Bijou, S. W., Peterson, R. F., & Ault, M. H. A method to integrate descriptive and experimental field studies at the level of data and empirical concepts. *Journal of Applied Behavior Analysis*, 1968, *1*, 175-191.

Hersen, M., & Bellack, A. S. *Behavioral assessment: A practical handbook.* Elmsford, N.Y.: Pergamon Press, 1976.

Johnson, S. M., & Bolstad, O. D. Methodological issues in naturalistic observation: Some problems and solutions for field research. In L. A. Hamerlynck, J. Handy, & D. A. Mash (Eds.), *Behavior change: Methodology, concepts, and practice.* Champaign, Ill.: Research Press, 1973.

Kazdin, A. E. Methodological and assessment considerations in evaluating reinforcement programs in applied settings. *Journal of Applied Behavior Analysis*, 1973, *6*, 517-531.

Repp, A. C., Roberts, D. M., Slack, D. J., Repp, C. F., & Berkler, M. S. A comparison of frequency, interval, and time-sampling methods of data collection. *Journal of Applied Behavior Analysis*, 1976, *9*, 501-508.

Review Set 10

1. F_____ counting measures the number of times a student performs a specific behavior within a set period of time.

2. I_____ r_____ is a measure of the degree to which two or more observers agree that a specific behavior occurred.

3. Reliability between observers is especially important when a behavior is highly d_____ or when a highly a_____ procedure is being used.

4. One method of calculating interobserver reliability is to divide the number of times the observers a_____ that the behavior occurred by the number of times they a_____ plus the number of times they d_____, and multiply by 100.

5. Another method of calculating interobserver reliability when frequency records are collected is to divide the l_____ number recorded by the h_____ number recorded, and multiply by 100.

6. The minimum interobserver reliability percentage that is acceptable is above _____.

7. A g_____ offers a visual representation of the effectiveness of a treatment program.

8. In t_____ s_____ recording the student is observed at fixed intervals for a specified period of time to determine whether or not a specific behavior occurred during each observation interval.

9. The rule to follow in order to avoid biasing time sampling records is: the student should have at least the same number of opportunities each observation session to misbehave during t_____ as during the b_____.

10. To judge the effectiveness of each reduction procedure, a c_____ must be set.

The answers are on page 177.

CHAPTER 11

The Development of Lasting Programs: Generalization, Maintenance of the Treatment Effect, Program Pitfalls, and Guidelines for Establishing Behavioral Programs

You learned how to measure and evaluate the results of your reduction programs in the last two chapters. Now, in this chapter, we'll consider four other important concerns regarding behavioral reduction programs: generalization of the reductive effect, maintenance of the behavior reduction, potential programming pitfalls, and guidelines for establishing effective reduction programs. Generalization training and the maintenance of behavior reduction will be discussed first because scientific evidence indicates that reductions in a student's misbehaviors don't automatically transfer to new settings and situations or remain after the termination of the behavioral program. Thus, because the inhibition of your student's misbehavior is likely to be situation specific, you should learn how to program for generalization and the maintenance of the reductive effect. We'll then consider some of the pitfalls you must avoid in order to ensure that your behavioral programs are successful, and conclude with a discussion of some useful guidelines you may follow to help ensure that your behavioral reductive programs are humane, ethical, beneficial, enduring, and successful.

GENERALIZATION TRAINING

Generalization training is a procedure for transferring control over behavior in one situation to other situations.

When a student's misbehavior has been eliminated in one situation or setting, we also want it to be absent in others. When this occurs, we say that generalization has taken place. Unfortunately, students rarely spontaneously stop misbehaving in untreated settings or situations. Thus, behavior reductions achieved in the classroom don't automatically transfer to the home, reductions produced in a one-to-one situation don't automatically transfer to a group situation, and the success of one instructor in eliminating the misbehavior doesn't automatically transfer to another. A major reason generalization rarely occurs is that most students, even the most severely intellectually impaired, can *discriminate* between situations and settings such as between home and the classroom, one-to-one situations and group situations, and different instructors. As a result, if we want generalization to occur, we must program for it. The means by which we do this is called generalization training.

Generalization training can be accomplished either during or after a behavioral program. Thus, you can implement generalization training while you are reducing the misbehavior or after the misbehavior has been eliminated. There are several ways of facilitating generalization.

Emphasize common elements between new settings and the original treatment setting. You can help your students learn to generalize by ensuring that the discriminative stimuli and aversive consequences from the original setting are present in the new settings. For instance, if you want a student to not disrobe at home, make sure that her parents have set up a timeout area in the home and that they use the word *no* and place her in timeout in the same manner as you did at school.

Reduce the misbehavior under a variety of conditions. The more conditions in which the misbehavior is reduced, the more likely it is that it won't occur in new situations. For instance, if you want to decrease the likelihood that the student will grab her food with her hands at home, have several different classroom instructors treat food grabbing in several different situations at school, such as while the student is alone, sitting at a table with others, or in different rooms. Research has indicated that generalization of the reductive effect is more likely to occur when several different instructors treat the student's misbehavior in several different situations or settings.

Use conditioned aversive stimuli in the original treatment situation. In this way natural consequences, rather than artificial ones, are controlling the student's misbehavior. By doing this you can greatly facilitate the generalization process and maintenance of the suppression effect as well. For example, you should pair the word *no* with the delivery of the aversive consequence, since it's likely that the student will be told *no* when she misbehaves in just about any setting, whereas she may not always receive the particular consequence that you were using.

MAINTENANCE OF BEHAVIORAL REDUCTION

No matter how effective your behavioral procedure was in decreasing an undesirable behavior, its significance is meaningless if the undesirable behavior returns once the procedure is discontinued. To ensure that this doesn't happen, we must be concerned about maintaining the effect of our intervention. We can never assume that the effect will be maintained after the program is withdrawn; consequently, we must program for the maintenance of the reductive effect.

There are several procedures that can be used to increase the likelihood that the misbehavior will not return. Note that there's little difference between these procedures and the procedures that facilitate generalization training. (In fact, some of the same procedures are used in both cases.) This is because our concerns regarding maintenance of the behavioral reduction and generalization training are so closely related.

Substitute naturally occurring reinforcers for the artificial or programmed reinforcers that were used to reinforce alternative appropriate behaviors. Although artificial reinforcers are often necessary to effectively increase appropriate behavior or reinforce the absence of misbehavior, they should be phased out once the behavior is occurring at the desired level and more natural reinforcers should be substituted. Furthermore, the use of artificial reinforcers together with the natural reinforcer may, in fact, enhance the subsequent effectiveness of the natural reinforcer. For example, the simultaneous use of an edible and praise when reinforcing the absence of screaming increases the likelihood that the praise (or attention) alone will reinforce quiet. Or praise can be used to reinforce squeezing a ball (an incompatible behavior that is being reinforced) and then gradually be eliminated as the student begins squeezing the ball. At that point, the natural reinforcer (the tactual stimulation that follows the correct response, ball squeezing) may be sufficient to maintain this incompatible behavior.

Train other individuals in the student's life, such as relatives or residential caretakers, to carry out your behavioral program. To ensure that the reduction of the student's misbehaviors will be maintained at home, over the summer, during other shifts, or in his new classroom during the coming school year, you should train "significant others" to carry out your successful behavioral program in other settings. This point can't be stressed enough, since research has shown that autistic and retarded children whose parents were trained in behavioral reductive techniques misbehaved very little or not at all at home, whereas similar children who were institutionalized in facilities where the staff members were untrained in the treatment techniques regressed and their misbehaviors returned. Another way of looking at this finding is that *students don't regress, programs do!*

Gradually introduce a delay in providing the behavioral consequences so that they don't have to be delivered immediately. The less immediate the reductive consequences, the more the student will be prepared for normalization, that is, functioning under the same types of contingencies and consequences as normal persons. This is important because the real world provides fewer immediate behavioral consequences.

With severely and profoundly retarded students, it's probable that you won't be delaying the behavioral consequences for some time. However, there is a way to do so through the use of a bridging stimulus. A bridging stimulus serves to connect the time between the performance of a behavior and the delivery of the consequence. In effect, it "bridges" the time period. For instance, you could use a bridging stimulus with a wheelchair-bound student who is being phased into a "more normal" classroom and who grabs other students. It would be important for this student to learn that his grabbing still would be punished in his new classroom, even though the ratio of staff to students made it impossible to punish grabbing immediately. To use a bridging stimulus in this case, the student could be wheeled to a corner of the room where he would wait until an instructor had the time to implement the reductive consequence. By being taken to the same corner each time, he would begin to associate it with the delivery of the punisher, since the corner would bridge the time period between the misbehavior and the delivery of the punisher. Eventually the corner itself should acquire punishing properties because of its repeated association or pairing with the punisher. Although it's doubtful that you'll be using this technique in the near future, you should be aware of it so that you can utilize it when it's needed.

Vary the treatment conditions. This will keep the student from discriminating when a negative consequence is likely to occur. The best way to prevent the student from discriminating, that is, picking up cues regarding when and where the negative consequences will be delivered and by whom, is to treat the behavior in a variety of settings with several individuals delivering the consequences. This, of course, constitutes generalization training. It's especially important in punishment or aversive programs that you ensure that a number of individuals are associated with the program. Otherwise the misbehavior will be reduced or eliminated only in the presence of those few individuals who participated in the program.

PROGRAMMING PITFALLS

There are several pitfalls that you should avoid as you establish and carry out your behavioral programs. You can avoid these pitfalls as follows.

Don't attempt to reduce or eliminate highly disruptive behaviors until you become thoroughly proficient as a behavior change agent. Rather, work with simple misbehaviors and problems until you have achieved a sufficient amount of expertise. It takes years to develop good surgeons and behavior modifiers.

Don't change a program or drop it until you've thoroughly analyzed why it may not be working. Some factors to consider in your analysis are:

1. Does the student know what is expected of her? You can answer this question for nonverbal students by making sure that the negative consequences immediately follow the misbehavior. For verbal students, simply tell them that the negative consequences will follow their misbehavior or ask them to tell you what will happen to them the next time they misbehave.

2. Do all of the change agents in the environment (all instructors, parents, and volunteers) understand the program that you are using? You should make sure that everyone is very familiar with the program. Never set up a program without informing everyone of what you are doing and gaining their cooperation to help you with the program.

3. Are all of the change agents motivated to participate in the program and help make it work? Often change agents aren't motivated to participate or agree to participate in a program when they don't feel adequately informed or involved. By involving them early in the design of the intervention, you'll avoid the problems of apathy and sabotage and gain their willingness to make the necessary sacrifices to ensure the success of your program.

4. Are the negative consequences working as they should? If it appears that they're not, you should evaluate and possibly change the following variables: the type of consequence being used, the amount or duration of the consequence being delivered, the immediacy with which the consequence is delivered, and the aversiveness of the consequence for the student.

5. Is the program being applied consistently and correctly? Failure to consistently apply the program is probably the most common reason programs fail to reduce behavior.

GUIDELINES FOR ESTABLISHING PROGRAMS

You've now learned the behavioral principles in this book and are ready to apply them with your students. However, before you do, carefully consider the following suggestions and guidelines. Once you have, you should be ready to begin effectively decreasing the undesirable behaviors of your students.

Know thyself. Don't consider changing the behavior of others until you've gained some insight into your own behavior. Understanding why you behave as you do will help you become a proficient and humane behavior modifier.

Know the student. You should always strive to learn as much about your students as possible. And the only way to learn about them is to work directly with them. This is an especially important concern for professionals who are responsible for designing programs. You can't design an effective program for a student unless you've spent sufficient time observing him prior to writing up the program. Knowing your students' strengths and weaknesses will ensure that they are developmentally ready to benefit from whatever interventions you have selected for them.

Know that the program will be beneficial for the student. No program should be used simply because it will make the student less annoying or inconvenient to work with. Rather, a reductive program should only be used if it will further the student's progress toward a normal, productive life.

Develop a value system that respects the dignity of the student and that operates on the principle of fairness. Our students deserve fairness and respect just as does everyone. You will be demonstrating that you are fair and respect the student if you (1) don't apply procedures arbitrarily, (2) don't refuse to use a procedure simply because of a personal bias, such as refusing to use a timeout procedure simply because you don't believe in using it,

(3) always attempt to use a systematic approach in modifying the student's behavior and evaluate that approach, (4) don't refuse to seek help from others because you think that such assistance would make you appear incompetent, (5) systematically evaluate your own performance from time to time to ensure that you are correctly carrying out the various procedures you're using with your students, and (6) always attempt to use the least restrictive reductive procedure that the treatment literature has shown to be effective. Only consider using a more restrictive procedure if the initial one proves to be ineffective.

Keep everyone informed about your programs. If your program is well designed and based on sound behavioral principles, then there's no cause for concern when you inform a student's parents, guardians, advocate, or the facility administration about what you intend to do. As noted previously, it's imperative that you seek informed consent when you're considering the use of aversive procedures to decrease a student's undesirable behaviors. However, it's also a good idea to keep all concerned parties abreast of all your various programs even if they are nonaversive, for example, using a DRI procedure. By doing so, you'll be demonstrating your competence and concern for your students.

It's fitting that this book end with the statement that any system can be misused and abused by the individuals who are responsible for implementing it. Knowledge is power and people with power must take the responsibility to use it in beneficial ways. Behavioral reductive techniques are powerful procedures that can be useful or damaging depending on how they are used. You now have the power to decrease behavior with behavioral techniques and the responsibility to use that power wisely.

SUMMARY

For reductive programs to be considered successful, reductions of misbehaviors must be maintained in a variety of situations and settings long after the initial intervention is terminated. Unfortunately, this doesn't happen automatically, so generalization and maintenance of behavior reduction also must be programmed. Generalization training is the way that control over behavior in one situation is transferred to other situations. Several ways of facilitating generalization are emphasizing the common elements between new settings and the original one; reducing the misbehavior under a variety of conditions; and using conditioned aversive stimuli in the original treatment situation.

Behavior maintenance is an integral part of generalization training, so the procedures for both are very similar. Some maintenance procedures are substituting natural reinforcers for the artificial ones used to reinforce alternative appropriate behaviors; training other individuals in the student's life to carry out your program; gradually delaying the delivery of behavioral consequences; and varying the treatment conditions.

Two major pitfalls should be avoided in carrying out behavioral programs: (1) attempting to reduce or eliminate highly disruptive behaviors before you have developed sufficient proficiency as a behavior change agent and (2) changing or discontinuing a program that isn't working without first analyzing why it failed.

Finally, there are several suggested guidelines for establishing effective and humane programs. They include (1) understanding your own behavior as a prerequisite to understanding your students' behavior, (2) learning as much as possible about each student by working directly with her, (3) only choosing those programs that further the student's progress toward a normal and productive life, (4) developing a value system that respects the student's dignity and is fair, and (5) keeping all interested parties informed about your programs.

SUGGESTED READINGS

Birnbrauer, J. S. Mental retardation. In H. Leitenberg (Ed.), *Handbook of behavior modification and behavior therapy.* New York: Appleton-Century-Crofts, 1976.

Johnston, J. M., & Johnston, G. T. Modification of consonant speech–sound articulation in young children. *Journal of Applied Behavior Analysis*, 1972, *5*, 233-246.

Kazdin, A. E. *Behavior modification in applied settings* (Rev. ed.). Homewood, Ill.: Dorsey Press, 1980.

Marholin, D., II, Siegal, L. J., & Phillips, D. Treatment and transfer: A search for empirical procedures. In M. Hersen, R. M. Eisler, & P. M. Miller (Eds.), *Progress in behavior modification* (Vol. 3). New York: Academic Press, 1976.

Stokes, T. F., & Baer, D. M. An implicit technology of generalization. *Journal of Applied Behavioral Analysis*, 1977, *10*, 349-367.

Review Set 11

1. G_____ t_____ is a procedure designed to transfer the control over behavior in one situation to other situations.

2. The reason why generalization rarely occurs spontaneously is that students can d_____ between situations.

3. There are several ways of facilitating generalization training: (a) emphasize c_____ elements in the new setting that are shared with the original training setting, (b) reduce the misbehavior under a variety of c_____, (c) and use c_____ a_____ stimuli in the original treatment setting.

4. M_____ of b_____ r_____ and generalization training are closely related, since both are concerned with decreasing the likelihood that a misbehavior will occur in new situations.

5. There are several procedures that can be used to facilitate maintenance of behavioral reductions: (a) substitute n_____ occurring reinforcers for artificial ones, (b) t_____ other people in the student's life to carry out your program, (c) gradually introduce a d_____ in providing the behavioral consequences, and (d) vary the t_____ conditions.

6. A b_____ stimulus connects the time interval from the performance of a behavior to the delivery of the consequence.

7. There are two pitfalls to avoid when you attempt to establish or carry out a behavioral reduction program: (a) attempting to reduce highly d_____ behaviors before you have become thoroughly proficient as a behavior change agent, and (b) changing or dropping a program before you have thoroughly a_____ why it is not working.

8. There are several factors to consider when you analyze why a program is not working: (a) Does the student know what is e_____ of her? (b) Do all of the c_____ agents understand the program? (c) Are all of the change agents m_____ to participate in the program? (d) Are the n_____ consequences working as they should? and (e) Is the program being applied consistently and c_____?

9. The following are guidelines for establishing programs: know t_____, know the s_____, know that the p_____ will be beneficial for the student, develop a value system that respects the d_____ of the student and that operates on the principle of fairness, and keep everyone i_____ about your programs.

10. You will be demonstrating that you are fair and respect the student if you (a) don't apply procedures a_____, (b)

don't refuse to use a procedure because of a p_____
bias, (c) always attempt to use a s_____ approach in
modifying the student's behavior and evaluate that approach,
(d) don't refuse to seek help from o_____, (e) systematically evaluate your own p_____ periodically,
and (f) always attempt to use the l_____ restrictive
reductive technique that the treatment literature has shown
to be effective.

Answers are found on page 177.

APPENDIX A

Potential Reinforcers

EDIBLES
(Give very small pieces.)

Corn chips
Pretzel pieces
Cookies
Sugared cereals
Candy
Ice cream (spoonful from a cup)
Raisins
Peanuts

Pudding (spoonful from a cup)
Gelatin (spoonful from a cup)
Mini-marshmallows
Potato chips
Fruit (cherries, grapes, orange or apple slices)
Vegetable bits (carrot sticks, celery sticks)
Cheese (cubes, slices)
Popcorn

LIQUIDS
(Give in small sips or a squirt from a squirt bottle)

Colas, soft drinks
Orange drink, grape drink, cranberry drink
Fruit juices

Milk
Kool-Aid
Water
Decaffeinated coffee
Tea

OBJECTS

Dolls
Mechanical toys
Whistles (too large to be swallowed)
Bracelets
Hats
Rattles
Noisemakers

Colored chips (too large to be swallowed)
Stuffed toy animals
Balloons
Sweatshirts
Ribbons
Key chains
Decals
Balls

ACTIVITIES

Playing catch with the instructor
Playing on the swings
Playing on the jungle gym
Going on the merry-go-round
Running
Playing tag or hide-and-go-seek with the instructor
Going for a walk with the instructor
Playing with a pet
Taking an automobile ride
Swimming
Visiting the instructor's home
Looking through a book or magazine that has colored pictures
Playing in the gym (unstructured play)
Hearing music
Riding on a rocking horse
Finger painting
Playing in a wading pool
Smelling different fragrances
Opening jars with an edible inside
Jumping
Lying on a waterbed
Clapping hands

SOCIAL PRAISE

"Good" or "Good boy or girl."
"Very good."
"I like that."
"That's good."
"I'm glad you did that."
"That's right, ___(name)___."
"You did a good ___(thing)___."
"Good ___(job)___."
"Mmm-hmm."
"Fine."
"You did it. Very good."
"Thank you" or "Thank you very much."
"I'm so happy with you."
"I'm proud of you."

NONVERBAL MESSAGES AND MOVEMENTS

Facial Expressions

Smiling
Showing surprise and delight
Nodding your head in an approving manner
Laughing
Winking

Being Near the Student

Standing near the student
Sitting near the student

Physical Contact

Hugging
Patting
Touching the student's arm
Tickling
Bouncing the student on your knees

Rubbing the student's back
Kissing
Picking the student up
Wrestling
Tousling the student's hair

Playing patty-cake
Holding the student
Holding the student's hand
Touching the student with a
  vibrator

APPENDIX B

Selected Journals

The following list contains journals that regularly publish articles on the use of behavior modification with retarded students.

American Journal of Mental Deficiency. Washington, D.C.: American Association on Mental Deficiency.

Analysis and Intervention in Developmental Disabilities. Elmsford, N.Y.: Pergamon Press, Inc.

Behavior Modification. Beverly Hills, Calif.: Sage Publications.

Behavior Research of Severe Developmental Disabilities. Amsterdam: North-Holland Publishing Co.

Behavior Therapy. New York: Association for Advancement of Behavior Therapy.

Behaviour Research and Therapy. Elmsford, N.Y.: Pergamon Press, Inc.

Child Behavior Therapy. New York: The Haworth Press.

Education and Training of the Mentally Retarded. Reston, Va.: Division on Mental Retardation, The Council for Exceptional Children.

Education and Treatment of Children. Pittsburgh, Pa.: Pressley Ridge School.

Exceptional Children. Reston, Va.: The Council for Exceptional Children.

Journal of Applied Behavior Analysis. Lawrence, Kans.: Society for the Experimental Analysis of Behavior, Inc.

Journal of Autism and Developmental Disorders. New York: Plenum Publishing Corp.

Journal of Behavior Therapy and Experimental Psychiatry. Elmsford, N.Y.: Pergamon Press, Inc.

Journal of Learning Disabilities. Chicago: The Professional Press, Inc.

162   Selected Journals

Journal of School Psychology. New York: The Journal of School Psychology, Inc.

The Journal of Special Education. New York: Grune & Stratton, Inc.

The Journal of the Association for the Severely Handicapped. Seattle: The Association for the Severely Handicapped.

Mental Retardation. Washington, D.C.: American Association on Mental Deficiency.

Teaching Exceptional Children. Reston, Va.: The Council for Exceptional Children.

APPENDIX C

Answers for
Practice and Review Sets

1. Least Restrictive Treatment Model
2. litigation
3. a. baseline
   b. literature
   c. least
   d. accurate
   e. more, less
   f. parents, human rights, administrator
4. three

Practice Set 2A

1. 10 seconds
2. No. Mr. Ryan would be reinforcing Karen's blouse ripping as well as her not screaming. It would be best to wait for the next interval of nonscreaming to elapse.
3. a. Select a time period each day that can be completely devoted to the program.
   b. One person in the family should take responsibility for the program.
   c. Create activities that are as incompatible as possible with the inappropriate behavior.
4. Advantages:
   a. It's a simple procedure.
   b. It works directly on the misbehavior.

163

Disadvantages:

a. It doesn't teach an appropriate behavior.

b. There's a risk of reinforcing some other type of misbehavior.

5. Physical contact. Physical contact appears to be Dante's most preferred reinforcer and as such should be tried first.

Practice Set 2B

1. Ms. Goldman should pick a behavior that Teddy already performs. Thus, she would pick either having Teddy look at her when instructed or having him hand her objects. She would not pick pointing at objects because he doesn't at this time perform that behavior.

2. Advantage:

It increases an appropriate behavior.

Disadvantages:

a. It doesn't work directly on the misbehavior.

b. The misbehavior can still occur during the program.

3. Mr. Henson could consider instituting a DRA program. He was initially using a DRO procedure.

Practice Set 2C

1. 1-c

2-e

3-f

4-b

5-d

6-a

2. Advantage:

The inappropriate behavior can't occur when the incompatible behavior is occurring.

Disadvantage:

They may have trouble, on occasion, finding socially and educationally appropriate incompatible behaviors.

3. DRI. The severity of the misbehavior dictates that it be reduced as soon as possible. DRI would be the best procedure because it guarantees that the misbehavior can't occur when the reinforced behavior is occurring. In other words, DRI of-

Answers   **165**

fers the tightest form of reinforcement control over the self-abusive behavior.
4. a. DRO
   b. DRI
   c. DRA
   d. DRI
   e. DRO
   f. DRA

Review Set 2

1. DRO
2. half, short
3. simple
4. directly
5. appropriate, inappropriate
6. behaviors
7. DRA
8. RAB
9. inappropriate
10. appropriate
11. inappropriate, directly
12. DRI, incompatible
13. RIB
14. inappropriate
15. incompatible
16. time, person, incompatible
17. reinforcer
18. performs
19. DRI

Practice Set 3A

1. Satiation could reasonably be tried for stealing toys, hoarding toys, rocking, and banging a table with toys. The satiation procedure for rocking would involve providing the student with a rocking chair, while toy banging could be satiated by providing the student with a toy that involves banging, e.g., a Fischer-Price hammer set. All of the other misbehaviors are too serious in nature to consider treating them by satiation.

2. Since the client is apparently reinforced by collecting and hoarding his dirty clothes, Ms. Harris could try placing as much of the unit's dirty laundry in his closet as possible. When his closet becomes filled with dirty clothes, the client may very well stop hoarding his dirty clothes.

3. Let Travis eat as much as he wants to at lunch. You'll want to keep accurate records of his weight and how much food he consumes at lunch. If Travis is full (satiated), he should be less motivated to engage in rumination.

Practice Set 3B

1. Negative practice could reasonably be tried for self-stimulating, paper tearing, and running away. The other misbehaviors listed are too serious in nature to consider treating them with negative practice.

2. Mr. Parsons should require Jackie to repeatedly practice pulling grass and plants whenever he discovers her exhibiting this behavior. He should ensure that the negative practice requires enough physical effort to make it aversive and should guide Jackie rapidly if she refuses to pull weeds or pulls them too slowly. Also, he should use a DRO program to reinforce the absence of plant pulling. To avoid damaging the grounds, Mr. Parsons should select a place full of weeds as the site for the negative practice sessions.

3. Negative Practice:
   a. Follows the misbehavior (it is a consequence)
   b. Deals with the response
   c. Is an aversive and intrusive procedure

   Satiation:
   a. Is given independent of the misbehavior
   b. Deals with the reinforcer
   c. Is a nonaversive and nonintrusive procedure

Review Set 3

1. satiation
2. noncontingently
3. following
4. nonaversive
5. eliminate
6. temporary
7. few
8. negative practice

9. negative practice, satiation
10. long, reduced
11. physically, control
12. combative
13. misbehavior, undesirable
14. independently, manual guidance

Practice Set 4

1. Extinction could be tried for masturbating, whining, pestering, out-of-seat behavior, or cursing. The other behaviors listed are too serious in nature to consider treating them with extinction. Self-stimulatory behaviors would not be appropriate candidates for an extinction procedure because typically they are not maintained by an external reinforcer such as attention.
2. The teacher should ignore Dick when he seeks attention by stepping between her and another student.
3. You would tell Ms. Kelly not to worry because Conrad's behaviors are very characteristic of what happens when a student is placed on extinction. Simply tell her that if she persists, Conrad will stop whining and aggressing.
4. The advantages of extinction are that it is (1) straightforward when conducted properly, (2) effective in eliminating the undesirable behavior, (3) long lasting, and (4) relatively nonaversive.
5. The disadvantages of extinction are that (1) the behavior may initially increase in frequency and intensity, (2) it requires a consistent approach, (3) it takes time to work, (4) the student may become aggressive, (5) it's sometimes difficult to identify the reinforcer, (6) the schedule of reinforcement for the undesirable behavior is unknown, so the length of time necessary for extinction to be effective is unknown, and (7) it can't be used for dangerous or highly disruptive behaviors.

Review Set 4

1. extinction
2. worse, better, gradually, aggression, spontaneous recovery
3. eliminate, long
4. simple, consistency
5. nonaversive, 2

Practice Set 5

1. Assuming that it was necessary, physical restraint could be used for rectal digging, hitting others, throwing objects, and face scratching. The other behaviors listed are usually treatable by less restrictive methods.

2. a. Behavioral physical restraint is a negative consequence, whereas custodial physical restraint is often applied independent of any misbehavior. Thus, behavioral restraint serves a programmatic function whereas custodial restraint serves a custodial function.

   b. The duration of behavioral physical restraint is prespecified, whereas the duration of custodial physical restraint is not specified.

   c. The duration of behavioral physical restraint is brief, usually no more than 30 minutes, whereas custodial physical restraint can last indefinitely.

3. Laura's teacher could restrain her hands with his for a prespecified period following each instance of self-abuse.

4. Laura's teacher could restrain her arms by placing a splint-like device over them contingent on self-abuse.

5. Any physical contact associated with the restraint procedure could become reinforcing for a student who has been deprived of physical contact. The use of physical contact to reinforce an appropriate behavior provides the student with an acceptable means of obtaining physical contact.

Review Set 5

1. physical restraint
2. self-abusive
3. behavioral, custodial
4. manually, mechanically
5. increase, touch, mechanical
6. can't, eliminated, long
7. aversive, reinforcing, exercise, punitive, staff, physically
8. document, permission
9. trained

1. Type I, the application of an aversive event (spanking) following the misbehavior (biting little sister)

2. Type II, the withdrawal of a positive reinforcer, because Alice missed a number of reinforcing events, e.g., playing outside or watching TV, while she was in her room

3. Sending Robert to the corner is not a punishing consequence because it has not decreased his hitting behavior. Ms. Ryan has learned that you describe a consequence by its effect on the behavior. In this case, sending Robert to the corner may even be a reinforcing consequence that is maintaining his hitting.

4. Always provide reinforcement for an alternative appropriate behavior.

5. The four variables that influence the effectiveness of a punishment procedure are immediacy, intensity, the schedule of punishment, and whether or not an alternative appropriate behavior is reinforced.

Practice Set 6B

1. Punishment:
   a. May immediately suppress behavior
   b. May produce a long-lasting effect
   c. May produce complete suppression of the behavior
   d. May affect the behavior of other students in that they will avoid engaging in the misbehavior they saw being punished
   e. May produce an irreversible effect

2. Punishment:
   a. May produce emotional behavior
   b. May cause the student to become aggressive
   c. May produce negative modeling
   d. May cause the student to avoid or escape punishing situations or people

3. operant, elicited

4. A conditioned aversive stimulus

5. When he bangs the table with his fists. That response occurs early in the behavior chain and thus is weakly linked with whatever terminal reinforcer is maintaining the running away behavior chain. This also prevents any continuation of the chain and its effects.

Review Set 6

1. punishment
2. application
3. withdrawal, positive reinforcer
4. reinforcement, alternative appropriate
5. consequence, effect
6. immediately, long-lasting, complete, others, irreversible
7. emotional, aggression, negative, escape, avoid
8. conditioned aversive
9. terminal

Practice Set 7A

1. Exclusionary timeout involves removing the student from the reinforcers (reinforcing environment), whereas nonexclusionary timeout involves removing the reinforcers from the student while he remains in the reinforcing environment.
2. The timeout interval should be extended in 1-minute blocks of time until the student is quiet during the last 15 seconds of a minute.
3. exclusionary timeout
4. high density
5. reinforcement
6. duration, brief
7. misbehaving
8. immediately
9. neutral, *no*
10. bootleg
11. records
12. written permission

Practice Set 7B

1. a. timeout room
   b. timeout behind a partition
   c. timeout in the hallway
2. a. The student is removed from the reinforcing environment.
   b. The timeout room is devoid of any reinforcing stimuli.
   c. There's no possibility of bootleg reinforcement.

d. The student's presence in the room serves as a clear signal as to when timeout is in effect.

e. The timeout room provides a place to take highly agitated students and thereby minimizes the chance that they might injure someone or themselves, destroy property, or disrupt educational activities.

3. a. Timeout cannot be implemented immediately.

b. A special room is required.

c. Attention may be given to the misbehaving student on the way to the timeout room.

d. The continuity of classroom educational tasks is interrupted when the staff person leaves to implement timeout.

e. It's difficult to program for generalization, since the success of this procedure depends on the availability of a timeout room.

f. It may not be effective for self-isolates, high rate self-stimulators, or frequent masturbators.

g. The student's misbehavior in timeout could force the instructor to intervene and thereby nullify the timeout procedure.

h. There is the remote possibility that the procedure could be used in an arbitrary or punitive fashion by staff.

4. The disadvantage is that the student may receive bootleg reinforcement. The advantages include:

a. It usually can be implemented more quickly than the timeout room procedure.

b. It doesn't require a special room.

c. There's less interruption of the ongoing educational activities.

5. The two criteria include:

a. The student must be under good instructional control.

b. The timeout duration must be brief, usually 5 minutes or less.

The major disadvantage is that the student can run away or cause disturbances in other parts of the building.

Practice Set 7C

1. a. Withdrawing a specific reinforcer

b. Requiring the student to sit in a corner of the classroom

     c. Using the timeout ribbon procedure

2. a. Timeout can be implemented immediately.

     b. The student sees what he is missing.

     c. The presence or absence of the reinforcer provides a clear signal as to when timeout is in effect.

     d. No special room or area is required.

     e. There's little chance of bootleg reinforcement.

     f. There's little interruption of the classroom routine.

     g. The procedure can be used in a variety of locations and situations.

     h. There's less chance that the student will misbehave during timeout.

     i. It may be effective with self-isolates, self-stimulators, and masturbators.

     j. There's little chance that the procedure will be used in an arbitrary or punitive fashion.

3. a. The student may become combative or agitated.

     b. The student may disturb others.

     c. The specific reinforcer must be powerful and the student must be in a state of deprivation from that reinforcer.

4. a. A variety of misbehaviors can be treated.

     b. Positive modeling may occur.

     c. The student doesn't miss any ongoing educational activities.

5. a. The student may not stay in the timeout area.

     b. There is a greater chance of bootleg reinforcement and the procedure is less effective for self-isolates, self-stimulators, and masturbators.

6. a. Group treatment is possible.

     b. Bootleg reinforcement can be terminated quickly.

     c. Bizarre behavior during timeout can be interrupted and stopped.

     d. The presence or absence of the ribbon provides a clear signal to visitors as to when it's appropriate for them to interact with a student.

     e. The ribbon reminds the teacher to reinforce and to let the student out of timeout. It also helps in keeping track of who is currently in timeout.

     f. It can be used across settings.

g. The timed-out student doesn't have to be kept in one location.

7. The student can more easily disturb others or destroy property.

Review Set 7

1. timeout
2. exclusionary
3. nonexclusionary
4. false
5. timeout, partition, hallway
6. true
7. specific, timeout ribbon
8. chair
9. contingent observation
10. shorter
11. exclusionary, 3, 2

Practice Set 8A

1. overcorrection
2. true
3. false
4. false

Practice Set 8B

1. moment, moment
2. full
3. thumb, forefinger
4. shadowing
5. true
6. force, force
7. a. Require the spitter to apologize to others (spitting is annoying), clean the spat-upon object or person, and clean spittle from around his mouth. (Note: The spitter's teeth would not be brushed because no unhygienic oral contact would have occurred.)
   b. Require the window breaker to lie quietly on a bed or mat,

apologize to others (the others may have been annoyed or frightened), repair and clean windows, and medically treat anyone including himself who was injured by the broken glass.

c. Although no unhygienic oral contact occurs, require the ruminator to use an oral antiseptic to clean the vomitus from his mouth and freshen his breath.

d. Require the clothes ripper to lie quietly on a bed or mat, repair the torn garments, and repeatedly move his hands when instructed to do so.

e. Require the biter to lie quietly on a bed or mat, medicate his wounds, and brush his teeth with an oral antiseptic.

f. Require the clapper to repeatedly move his hands in one of three or four positions when instructed to do so and to hold each position for 15 seconds. No other type of overcorrection would be given since there was no environmental disruption.

g. Require the mouther to brush his teeth with an oral antiseptic because of unhygienic oral contact.

8. c
9. b

Review Set 8

1. punishment
2. directly, effort, immediately, rapidly
3. neutral
4. graduated guidance
5. full, partial, shadowing
6. verbal reprimand, timeout, verbal instructions, compliance
7. appropriate
8. reinforcement
9. complexity, time, intrusive
10. 3

Practice Set 9

1. a. 3 to 5, 4
   b. Yes
   c. Yes
   d. No. The baseline was sufficient because enough records

were taken to show that there were no wide fluctuations in Susan's operant level and the final data point was higher than the previous one, which meant that the behavior was not decreasing.

2. a. 0 to 2, 1.3
   b. Yes
   c. No
   d. Yes. The baseline should be continued until the last base-line data point is the same or higher than the previous day's data point. This is necessary because the purpose of the intervention will be to decrease the number of times Ross spits at his instructors.

3. 58.3% (7 ÷ 12 x 100)

4. a. 35 to 44, 38.8
   b. Yes
   c. Yes
   d. No. The baseline is sufficient for the same reasons specified in 1.

5. a. 14 to 70, 36.2
   b. No
   c. No
   d. Yes. The baseline should be continued until there are no wide fluctuations in Pat's percentage of finger flicking and the last baseline percentage is the same or higher than the previous day's percentage.

Review Set 9

1. operant level
2. baseline
3. objective
4. tally, frequency
5. time sampling
6. range, data point

Practice Set 10A

1. Yes. The baseline was stable and the final baseline day's data point was as high or higher than the previous day's.
2. Yes. The number of times Barbara hit her teachers decreased quickly and was ultimately reduced to zero.

3. Baseline average: 2.1 times per day (21 ÷ 10 = 2.1). Treatment average: .7 times per day (7 ÷ 10 = .7).
4. There was a 66.7% reduction in hitting during the timeout program (2.1 − .7 = 1.4; 1.4 ÷ 2.1 x 100 = 66.7%).
5. Yes. The treatment decreased Barbara's hitting by 66.7%, whereas the criterion level of success was a 60% reduction.
6. Yes
7. Baseline average: 2.71 times per day (19 ÷ 7 = 2.71). Treatment average: 3.1 times per day (31 ÷ 10 = 3.1).
8. No. The criterion level for success of a 60% decrease after 10 days was not reached. The graph shows that the 5-minute timeout program had no effect and, in fact, the misbehavior (pulling classmates' hair) actually increased.
9. She should increase the length of the timeout procedure, try a more restrictive procedure, or examine the program for problems and revise it.

Practice Set 10B

1. a. Yes
   b. Yes
2. a. 92%
   b. 8%
3. a. 60% $\dfrac{6\text{ agreements}}{6\text{ agreements} + 4\text{ disagreements}}$ x 100 = 60%
   b. Observer 1, 50%; Observer 2, 38.9%
4. 50%. Earl had 12 opportunities or intervals in which he could hand-flap and he did so in 6 of them. The 18 intervals in which overcorrection was in effect were subtracted out.
5. a. 96%
   b. 28%
   c. 70.8% (96 − 28 = 68; 68 ÷ 96 x 100 = 70.8%)
   d. Ms. Aaronoff should continue to use the DRI procedure since it reduced ear scratching by 70.8% of its baseline average, which was a much greater reduction than she had specified as meeting the criterion for success. She had stated that she would institute the physical restraint procedure only if the DRI procedure did not reduce ear scratching to 40% of its baseline average.

Review Set 10

1. frequency
2. interobserver reliability
3. disruptive (dangerous); aversive
4. agreed, agreed, disagreed
5. lower, higher
6. 70%
7. graph
8. time sampling
9. treatment, baseline
10. criterion

Review Set 11

1. generalization training
2. discriminate
3. common, conditions, conditioned aversive
4. maintenance of behavioral reduction
5. naturally, train, delay, treatment
6. bridging
7. disruptive, analyzed
8. expected, change, motivated, negative, correctly
9. thyself, student, program, dignity, informed
10. arbitrarily, personal, systematic, others, performance, least

GLOSSARY

Aversive stimulus: A stimulus that has the effect of decreasing a behavior when it is presented as a consequence of (contingent upon) that behavior. It is any stimulus that the individual will actively work to avoid.

Avoidance learning: The learning that occurs when a response is made in order to avoid or escape something that is unpleasant.

Baseline: The period of time during which a behavior is observed and measured without any intervention.

Behavior: Any observable and measurable act of the student. *See also* Response.

Behavior chain: A sequence of stimuli and responses that ends with a terminal reinforcer. It is also called a *stimulus-response chain*.

Behavior frequency: The number of times a behavior occurs during a specific period of time. *See also* Frequency counting.

Behavior maintenance: The degree to which a target behavior continues to occur or not occur after formal programming has been discontinued.

Behavioral approach: An approach to changing behavior based on direct observation and objective measurement of the student's behavior. It systematically uses methods and experimental findings from behavioral science.

Behavioral physical restraint: A procedure in which the student is prevented from moving his limbs and/or body for a prespecified period following the performance of a misbehavior. *See also* Physical restraint.

Behavioral repertoire: The behaviors that a particular student, at a particular time, is capable of performing.

Bootleg reinforcement: The reinforcement an individual receives (usually attention from peers) during a period in which no reinforcement is to be received (e.g., in timeout or extinction).

Bridging stimulus: A stimulus used to connect the time interval between the performance of the behavior and the consequence programmed to follow that behavior.

Conditioned aversive stimulus: A neutral stimulus that has acquired its aversive or punishing properties from being repeatedly paired with a punishing event.

Conditioned reinforcer: A previously neutral stimulus that has acquired its reinforcing properties from being repeatedly paired with a reinforcer.

Consequence: The event that happens to the student after the response occurs.

Contingency: The relation between the response (the target behavior) and the consequence.

Contingent observation: A type of nonexclusionary timeout in which the student sits on the perimeter of the room and observes others being reinforced for appropriate behavior during the timeout interval. *See also* Nonexclusionary timeout.

Contingent reinforcement: Reinforcement that depends upon a specific response.

Continuous recording: The recording of each behavior every time it occurs throughout the recording period.

Criterion level: The specification of how much a behavior is to be reduced. Criterion levels are used to evaluate the success of a behavioral reduction program.

Custodial physical restraint: A procedure in which the student is noncontingently prevented from moving his limbs and/or body for an unspecified period. It is commonly used in custodial facilities as an institutional convenience. *See also* Physical restraint.

Deprivation: The state that occurs when a reinforcer has been withheld for a while. It is the opposite of satiation.

Differential Reinforcement of Appropriate Behavior (DRA): A procedure in which a reinforcer is given following the performance of a prespecified appropriate behavior.

Differential Reinforcement of Incompatible Behavior (DRI): A procedure in which a reinforcer is given following the performance of a prespecified appropriate behavior that is physically and functionally incompatible with the targeted inappropriate behavior.

Differential Reinforcement of Other Behavior (DRO): A procedure in which a reinforcer is given at the end of a specified interval provided that a prespecified misbehavior has not occurred during the interval.

Discrimination: The process of behaving one way in one situation and a different way in another situation.

Discriminative stimulus: A stimulus that sets the occasion for a response to occur because it has been associated with reinforcement.

DRA: An abbreviation for Differential Reinforcement of Appropriate Behavior.

DRI: An abbreviation for Differential Reinforcement of Incompatible Behavior.

DRO: An abbreviation for Differential Reinforcement of Other Behavior.

Edible reinforcer: The foods preferred by the student.

Elicited aggression: The aggressive behavior directed toward anyone or anything except the source of punishment.

Exclusionary timeout: A Type II punishment procedure in which the misbehaving student is removed from the reinforcing environment for a specified period of time. The student can be taken to a timeout room, placed behind a partition, or required to stand in the hallway. *See also* Timeout.

Extinction: A procedure in which the reinforcer that has been sustaining or increasing an undesirable behavior is withheld.

Extinction-induced aggression: The aggressive behavior that accompanies the early phases of an extinction program.

Fading: The gradual removal of a prompt.

Frequency counting: A recording method in which the number of times a behavior occurs during a specified period of time is tallied.

Full graduated guidance: The segment of a graduated guidance procedure in which the trainer physically guides the performance of the desired behavior.

Generalization: The absence of a particular misbehavior in a situation in which treatment has not taken place.

Generalization training: A procedure for transferring control over behavior in one situation to other situations.

Graduated guidance: A technique combining physical guidance and fading in which the physical guidance is systematically and gradually reduced and faded according to the student's responsiveness. It has three parts: full graduated guidance, partial graduated guidance, and shadowing.

Incompatible behavior: A behavior that cannot be emitted simultaneously with another behavior because they are functionally and physically incompatible. It is also a behavior that interferes with the performance of another behavior. *See also* Differential Reinforcement of Incompatible Behavior.

Intermittent reinforcement: The reinforcement of some, but not all, occurrences of a response.

Interobserver reliability: A measure of the degree to which two or more observers agree that a specific behavior occurred.

Intervention: The action that is taken to change a target behavior.

Learning history: The sum of an individual's behaviors that have been conditioned or modified as a result of environmental events. It is also called a *reinforcement history*.

Least Restrictive Treatment Model: A list of the behaviorally based treatment procedures for decreasing the inappropriate behavior of retarded persons in which the procedures are ranked according to their aversiveness, severity, and intrusiveness.

Manual restraint: The use of physical contact, with the trainer's hands and/or body, in a behavioral physical restraint procedure. The restraint is contingent on the performance of a particular misbehavior.

Mechanical restraint: The use of devices such as straps or helmets in a behavioral physical restraint procedure. The noncontingent use of these devices is called custodial restraint.

Negative modeling: An undesirable side effect of punishment interventions whereby the punished person may imitate the punishing behavior of the person providing the punishment.

Negative practice: A procedure in which the misbehaving person is required to repeatedly practice her inappropriate behavior.

Noncontingent reinforcement: Reinforcement that is not related to any specific response.

Nonexclusionary timeout: A Type II punishment procedure in which the misbehaving student is allowed to remain in the reinforcing environment but is not allowed to engage in reinforcing activities for a specified period of time. It can be done by withdrawing a specific reinforcer, using contingent observation or a timeout chair, or instituting the timeout ribbon procedure. *See also* Timeout.

Operant aggression: The aggressive behavior directed toward the source of punishment.

Operant behavior: A behavior that is controlled by its consequences.

Operant level: A description of the frequency of a behavior before the intervention begins.

Overcorrection: A Type I punishment procedure in which the misbehaving student is required to overcorrect the environmental effects of her misbehavior and/or to practice appropriate forms of behavior in those situations in which the misbehavior commonly occurs.

Partial graduated guidance: The segment of a graduated guidance procedure in which the trainer fades the amount of physical guidance so that the student gradually performs the desired behavior with less assistance.

Physical restraint: A procedure in which the student is prevented from moving his limbs and/or body. There are two types, behavioral and custodial.

Positive reinforcement: The delivery of a positive reinforcer contingent upon a response or behavior.

Positive reinforcer: A stimulus that, when presented as a consequence of a behavior, results in an increase or maintenance of that behavior.

Punisher: Any event that decreases the future probability of the response it follows. It is also called a *punishing consequence.*

Punishing consequence: *See* Punisher.

Punishment: A procedure that decreases the future probability of a behavior. It has two forms, Type I and Type II.

R: An abbreviation for response.

Reinforcement: A procedure that maintains or increases the future probability of a behavior.

Reinforcement density: The frequency or rate at which responses are reinforced.

Reinforcement history: *See* Learning history.

Reinforcement schedule: *See* Schedule of reinforcement.

Reinforcer: Any event that maintains or increases the future probability of the response it follows. It is also called a *reinforcing consequence.*

Reinforcing consequence: *See* Reinforcer.

Reinforcing incompatible behaviors: *See* Differential Reinforcement of Incompatible Behavior.

Response: The behavior the student performs in the presence of a particular stimulus.

Response suppression: The reduction of a behavior following the presentation of an aversive stimulus.

Rumination: A maladaptive behavior in which the person regurgitates (vomits) and then either chews and reswallows the vomitus or expels it from his mouth. It can be life-threatening when the food is expelled, as the person may lose vital nutrients, or nonlife-threatening when the vomitus is reswallowed. It is generally considered to be a form of self-stimulation.

Satiation: A procedure in which a reinforcer that has been maintaining a misbehavior is presented noncontingently in unlimited amounts in order to reduce that behavior. Also, it is the state that occurs when a reinforcer has been presented to the point that it is no longer effective in increasing or maintaining a behavior. It is the opposite of deprivation.

Schedule of reinforcement: A description of when a reinforcer will be delivered. It is also called a *reinforcement schedule.*

S^D: An abbreviation for discriminative stimulus.

Shadowing: The segment of a graduated guidance procedure in which the amount of physical guidance has been faded to the point that the trainer has no physical contact with the student, but is prepared to reapply full or partial graduated guidance should the behavior slow down or stop.

Social reinforcer: A smile, praise, attention, or friendly remark that the student likes or enjoys.

Spontaneous recovery: The reappearance of a behavior that has been eliminated by means of an extinction procedure.

S^{r+}: An abbreviation for conditioned reinforcer.

S^{R+}: An abbreviation for terminal reinforcer.

Stimulus: Any physical object or occurrence in the environment that may set the occasion for a response to occur. Stimuli frequently used in behavioral programs include reinforcing stimuli, aversive stimuli, and discriminative stimuli.

Stimulus-response chain: *See* Behavior chain.

Target behavior: A desired behavior that does not occur or that occurs infrequently that we wish to establish or increase. It is also called a *terminal behavior.* In a behavioral reduction program, it is the inappropriate behavior that is to be decreased or eliminated.

Terminal behavior: *See* Target behavior.

Terminal reinforcer: The reinforcer at the end of a behavior (stimulus-response) chain.

Time sampling: A recording method in which the student is observed at fixed intervals (e.g., every 5 minutes) for a specified period of time (e.g., 30 seconds) and the occurrence or absence of a behavior during each interval is recorded.

Timeout: A Type II punishment procedure in which positive reinforcement is withdrawn for a prespecified period of time following the performance of a misbehavior. There are two types of timeout, exclusionary and nonexclusionary.

Timeout chair procedure: A type of nonexclusionary timeout in which the student sits in a chair in a corner of the room and observes others being reinforced for appropriate behavior during the timeout interval. *See also* Nonexclusionary timeout.

Timeout interval: The period of time that a timeout program is in effect following a prespecified undesirable behavior.

Timeout ribbon procedure: A nonexclusionary timeout procedure in which a student's ribbon (a conditioned reinforcer) is removed following a misbehavior. *See also* Nonexclusionary timeout.

Timeout room: A small room that is devoid of any reinforcing stimuli. *See also* Exclusionary timeout.

Type I punishment: The application of an aversive event following a misbehavior. *See also* Punishment.

Type II punishment: The withdrawal of a positive reinforcer following a misbehavior. *See also* Punishment.

INDEX

ABOUT THE AUTHOR

Photo by Lynn Sequoia Ellner

Dr. Foxx is Director of Treatment Development at the Anna Mental Health and Developmental Center in Anna, Illinois, and an adjunct professor in the Rehabilitation Institute at Southern Illinois University at Carbondale. He has written 4 books and dozens of scientific articles, and has made 12 training films on the use of behavioral principles to treat normal, retarded, emotionally disturbed, and autistic individuals. He also is the developer of the technique of overcorrection. Dr. Foxx has consulted at institutions, schools, and community-based facilities across the United States and in Canada, Great Britain, Puerto Rico, and Haiti. He is on the editorial board of eight scientific journals and is the consulting editor for Research Press special education publications. One of his books, *Toilet Training in Less Than a Day*, has sold over a million copies and has been translated into seven languages, and one of his training films, *Harry* (the treatment of a self-abusive man), has won numerous cinematic awards.